MW00647856

www.wadsworth.com

www.wadsworth.com is the World Wide Web site for Thomson Wadsworth and is your direct source to dozens of online resources.

At *www.wadsworth.com* you can find out about supplements, demonstration software, and student resources. You can also send email to many of our authors and preview new publications and exciting new technologies.

www.wadsworth.com
Changing the way the world learns®

Current Perspectives
Readings from InfoTrac® College Edition

American Government

THOMSON

™

WADSWORTH

Australia • Canada • Mexico • Singapore • Spain
United Kingdom • United States

THOMSON
™
WADSWORTH

Current Perspectives: Readings from InfoTrac® College Edition:
American Government

Publisher: *Clark Baxter*
Executive Editor: *David Tatom*
Assistant Editor: *Rebecca Green*
Editorial Assistant: *Cheryl Lee and Eva Dickerson*
Marketing Manager: *Janise Fry*
Marketing Assistant: *Teresa Jessen*
Advertising Project Manager: *Kelley McAllister*
Project Manager, Editorial Production: *Christy Krueger*

Creative Director: *Robert Hugel*
Print Buyer: *Karen Hunt*
Production Service: *Rozi Harris, Interactive Composition Corporation*
Permissions Editor: *Kiely Sisk*
Cover Designer: *Larry Didona*
Cover Image: *Photolibrary.com/Photonica*
Cover and Text Printer: *Thomson West*
Compositor: *Interactive Composition Corporation*

© 2006 Thomson Wadsworth, a part of The Thomson Corporation. Thomson, the Star logo, and Wadsworth are trademarks used herein under license.

ALL RIGHTS RESERVED. No part of this work covered by the copyright hereon may be reproduced or used in any form or by any means—graphic, electronic, or mechanical, including photocopying, recording, taping, Web distribution, information storage and retrieval systems, or in any other manner—without the written permission of the publisher.

Printed in the United States of America
1 2 3 4 5 6 7 09 08 07 06 05

For more information about our products, contact us at:
Thomson Learning Academic Resource Center
1-800-423-0563

For permission to use material from this text or product, submit a request online at http://www.thomsonrights.com. Any additional questions about permissions can be submitted by email to thomsonrights@thomson.com.

Library of Congress Control Number: 2004118223

ISBN 0-495-00798-6

Thomson Higher Education
10 Davis Drive
Belmont, CA 94002-3098
USA

Asia (including India)
Thomson Learning
5 Shenton Way
#01-01 UIC Building
Singapore 068808

Australia/New Zealand
Thomson Learning Australia
102 Dodds Street
Southbank, Victoria 3006
Australia

Canada
Thomson Nelson
1120 Birchmount Road
Toronto, Ontario M1K 5G4
Canada

UK/Europe/Middle East/Africa
Thomson Learning
High Holborn House
50-51 Bedford Row
London WC1R 4LR
United Kingdom

Latin America
Thomson Learning
Seneca, 53
Colonia Polanco
11560 Mexico
D.F. Mexico

Spain (including Portugal)
Thomson Paraninfo
Calle Magallanes, 25
28015 Madrid, Spain

Contents

1

Democracy and Political Theory

What Whitman Knew

David Brooks

Walt Whitman's "Democratic Vistas" is still the most trenchant explanation of American policies and ambitions.

Whenever I hear people say something stupid about America, which is often these days, I want to punch them in the nose and hand them Walt Whitman's 1871 essay "Democratic Vistas." The punch would temporarily stem the flow of idiocy, and the copy of "Democratic Vistas" would give them some accurate sense of what the United States is all about.

I should make it clear from the start that "Democratic Vistas" can be an infuriating piece of writing. Whitman could not be bothered with mundane considerations like clarity, coherence, and organizational logic. But it survives as our nation's most brilliant political sermon because it embodies the exuberant energy of American society—the energy that can make other peoples so nervous—and it captures in its hodgepodge nature both the high aspirations and the sordid realities of everyday life.

Whitman grappled with a central paradox: America strives to be great and powerful as a nation so that it can bring about the full flowering of individuals. "Political democracy, as it exists and practically works in America, with all its threatening evils, supplies a training school for making first-class men," he

The Atlantic Monthly, May 2003, v291, i4, p32–3.

© 2003 The Atlantic Monthly Magazine.

declared. "It is life's gymnasium, not of good only, but of all." Americans, he continued, are or should be "freedom's athletes," filled with "brave delight," audacious aims, and restless hopes.

Whitman longed for democratic noblemen and noblewomen who would be "in youth, fresh, ardent, emotional aspiring, full of adventure; at maturity, brave, perceptive, under control, neither too talkative nor too reticent, neither flippant nor somber; of the bodily figure, the movements easy, the complexion showing the best blood, somewhat flushed, breast expanded, an erect attitude, a voice whose sound outvies music, eyes of calm and steady gaze, yet capable also of flashing" These people would realize themselves amid political combat, hard work, social reform, nation building, and global causes: "So will individuality, and unimpeded branchings, flourish best under imperial republican forms."

The forces of affluence, fashion, comfort, modesty, and civility were, Whitman feared, breeding "inertness and fossilism" in his countrymen and countrywomen. He embraced, as countermeasures, spirit and vivacity in every form, no matter how vulgar. "I hail with joy the oceanic, variegated, intense practical energy, the demand for facts, even the business materialism of the current aged," he wrote. And he harbored the fervent hope that in the decades and centuries to come these raw energies would fuel spiritual and intellectual breakthroughs to create largeness of soul. "Thus we presume to write, as it were, upon things that exist not, and travel by maps yet unmade, and a blank. But the throes of birth are upon us."

A cosmic optimism pervades the essay, as it does all of Whitman's works. But "Democratic Vistas" was actually written in a mood of some bleakness. Whitman had believed that the Civil War would cleanse the nation of its most serious ills. As the war approached and then commenced, he railed against business interests and war opponents—and wrote several recruiting poems ("Thunder on! stride on, Democracy! strike with vengeful stroke!"). During the conflict he nursed the wounded. Literary critics sometimes emphasize the homoerotic nature of his attraction to the soldiers, but there was more to it than that. He admired their selfless heroism and their calmness and bravery as death approached. "Grand, common stock!" he exulted in "Democratic Vistas."

Whitman worked as a government clerk during the war, climbing from post to post, admiring Grant and worshipping Lincoln. Like everyone else, he had his moments of despair. "Every once in a while I feel so horrified & disgusted," he wrote to his mother in 1863. "[The war] seems to me like a great slaughter-house & the men mutually butchering each other." But even in such a dark moment, he continued, "I feel how impossible it appears again, to retire from this contest, until we have carried our points."

After the Union victory and Lincoln's sacrificial death, Whitman hoped that grief would cement the people together and call forth each person's best self. But of course the heroic mood did not survive. Life sank back to its normal sordid pattern. Political and business corruption were rampant. The middle classes returned to their trivial enjoyments.

In April of 1867 the prophetic British historian Thomas Carlyle published an essay called "Shooting Niagara—and After?" It was a vituperative attack on democracy, equality, and the liberation of the slaves. Where the common people rule, he argued, all culture is brought low, and life becomes mediocre and vulgar. Whitman took up his pen to defend democracy and the United States. But by the time he completed his reply, "Democratic Vistas," he had to admit that Carlyle was right on many points.

Whitman's essay contains vacillations that give it a head-spinning quality. One paragraph expresses revulsion over the people he saw around him.

> Never was there, perhaps, more hollowness at heart than at present, and here in the United States. Genuine belief seems to have left us . . . The spectacle is appalling. We live in an atmosphere of hypocrisy throughout. The men believe not in the women, nor the women in the men. A scornful superciliousness rules in literature. The aim of all the litterateurs is to find something to make fun of. A lot of churches, sects, etc., the most dismal phantasms I know, usurp the name of religion. Conversation is a mass of badinage.

The next paragraph recounts his walking the streets of New York, amid the "assemblages of the citizens in their groups, conversations, trades and evening amusements," and finding himself overcome by "exaltation" and "absolute fulfillment." In the paragraph after that he is despondent again, unable to find around him men worthy of the name, or arts worthy of appreciation. "A sort of dry and flat Sahara appears, these cities, crowded with petty grotesques, malformations, phantoms, playing meaningless antics."

Whitman was teaching an important lesson here: It is misleading to think one can arrive at a single, consistent judgment about the United States (or perhaps about any society). When it comes to the health of the country and its culture, the highest highs and the lowest lows are simultaneous and adjacent. Extremes must be accepted without regard for consistency—a lesson that our gloomy cultural critics and self-congratulatory political orators almost never get right.

In spite of his concessions to Carlyle, Whitman never fully reclined into pessimism. In the first place, his boundless energy always propelled him toward hopefulness, toward some activity that would lead to a brighter future. Second, unlike most cultural critics, he was not a snob, putting himself above those whose spiritual flatness he criticized. His love for his fellow Americans, as they actually lived and breathed around him, prevailed. No matter how trivial his neighbors might appear on the surface, he always saw through to their underlying nobility. "Shams, etc., will always be the show, like ocean's scum," he acknowledged. Even so, the American people were "the peaceablest and most good natured race in the world, and the most personally independent and intelligent." They were reliable in emergencies and possessed "a certain breadth of historic grandeur, of peace or war," in that regard surpassing the citizenry of any other great nation. The behavior of the average American during the Civil War, he contended, proved beyond all doubt "that popular democracy, whatever its faults and dangers, practically justifies itself beyond the proudest claims and wildest hopes of its enthusiasts." No future age could entirely know how the unknown rank and file of both armies fought and sacrificed for their ideals and proved themselves through "fearful tests."

Whitman had a remarkably subtle sense of America's unique historical mission.

Many people before and since have argued that the United States was assigned by God or destiny to spread democracy and advance human freedom around the globe. But Whitman learned, perhaps from Lincoln, that this is both a glorious and a tragic assignment. Reading "Democratic Vistas" is a bit like looking at a painting of the Annunciation, as Mary glimpses the divine but sad future of her son.

Whitman foresaw that the country's task of promoting liberty and democracy would be an arduous one. He further foresaw that we would have to embrace that task even at times when life at home was far from perfect. America's mission would not always be a romantic quest headed by dashing, heroic figures. It would sometimes be led by Presidents (and others) who failed to be impressive or inspirational. "Even today, amid these whirls, incredible flippancy, and blind fury of parties, infidelity, entire lack of first-class captains and leaders," the United States is still destined to sail the "dangerous sea," he argued. He wrote,

> It seems as if the Almighty had spread before this nation charts of imperial destinies, dazzling as the sun, yet with many a deep intestine difficulty, and human aggregate of cankerous imperfection . . . You said in your soul, I will be empire of empires, overshadowing all else, past and present, putting the history of Old-World dynasties, conquests behind me, as of no account—making a new history, a history of democracy, making old history a dwarf—I alone inaugurating largeness, culminating time.

Whitman also perceived that the nation could not readily communicate its mission, either to the world or to itself. He dreamed that a crop of literary giants would emerge to develop an American soul equal to American economic and political might. "Democratic Vistas" was intended to inspire a "literatus of the modern"—poets and writers who would complete the task Whitman had begun.

It's hard these days to put that much faith in poets and writers. The geniuses Whitman envisioned have not arrived. America's greatest contributions to the world are generally found in its innovations and its actions, not in literary masterpieces. Now, more than 130 years after Whitman published "Democratic Vistas" that essay remains the best explanation of the nation's energy and aspirations.

No one since Whitman has captured quite so well the motivating hopefulness that propels American policy and makes the nation a great and restless force in the world. No other essay communicates quite so well what it is like to live constantly in the shadow of the future, trusting that tomorrow's world will be better and will redeem the incompleteness of the present. Whitman's essay, with its nuanced understanding of the American national character, stands today as a powerful rebuttal to, for example, the parades of European anti-Americans. What these groups despise is a cliche—a flat and simple-minded image of American power. They do not see, as Whitman did, that despite its many imperfections, America is a force for democracy and progress. "Far, far indeed, stretch, in distance, our Vistas!" Whitman wrote. "How much is still to be disentangled, freed!"

CRITICAL THINKING QUESTIONS

1. How did Whitman's "Democratic Vistas" point out both the good and bad aspects of American democracy?
2. In what ways was the essay both optimistic and pessimistic about America and democracy?
3. What connection does Whitman draw between America's ideals at home and a mission to promote democracy and liberty abroad?
4. In what ways is the United States a force for "democracy and progress" in the world? In what ways does it do the opposite?

2

The Constitution

The Organic and Moral Elements in the American Constitution

Paul Johnson

The Constitution is a product of colonial experience under British common law and other historic traditions.

In the endless human adventure of self-government, the United States has been one of the great stories of success. The explanation for this must lie primarily in its constitution and, still more, in its constitutionalism—that is, its capacity to modify its mode of government by due process rather than by violence. Nowadays the study of constitutions is regarded as dull work; "constitutional history" is completely out of fashion. Yet constitutions are important. No other document tells us more about a country, or why its public system works or does not work. The United States has had the same constitution for 200 years. In the same period, another highly sophisticated and civilized country, France, has tried a dozen, some abortive; only under the Fifth Republic has it acquired a satisfactory document, likely to become permanent. How did the United States manage to get it right the first time?

The question is all the more worth asking if we reflect that the American statesmen of the 1770s and 1780s really inaugurated the constitutional era in

World and I, Feb 2003, v18, i2.

© 2003 News World Communications, Inc.

world history. During the last two centuries, the number of written constitutions framed, debated, adopted, scrapped, and recast runs into thousands. Many, like those of the Central African Republic and the United Arab Republic, have simply failed. Others, like the Soviet constitution, are dead letters, quite meaningless to those who have to live under them. In the last forty years alone over a hundred new nations have come into existence, the great majority of them with constitutions that are rhetorical rather than real. While expressed in noble and beautiful language, their provisions bear no relation to the way in which the regimes that hold power actually behave. The United States is the only major country to have survived two centuries of this disillusioning era—including its own appalling civil war—with its founding code substantially intact, honored by its rulers and respected by its citizens.

ROOTS OF AMERICAN POLITICAL ORDER

The reasons for this success are twofold. The American Constitution sprang not from a vacuum but from a rich and varied complex of traditions, some of them very old. Because of this origin, it was able to develop a creative life of its own, responding to new challenges not only by deliberative enactment but by organic growth. It proved a living thing because it came from living soil.

Three elements influenced the political thinking of American public men in the last quarter of the eighteenth century. The first was the comparatively new stress upon equality and human rights generated by the French writers of the Enlightenment—Rousseau, Diderot, and the other Encyclopaedists. They were responsible for what might be called the utopian element in the new American polity, the belief that a perfect society could be created afresh. Without their influence, the first two paragraphs of the Declaration of Independence would not have been phrased as they were; nor would the actual Constitution itself, with its deliberate attempt to achieve a separation of powers, have been so systematic.

The principal formative element, however, was the English common law tradition and its use by English parliamentarians, over the centuries, to curb the royal power. Men like John Adams and Thomas Jefferson wrote and deliberated within the historical framework of the British Constitution. To be sure, it was largely unwritten, though punctuated by key statutes like Magna Carta, the Bill of Rights, and Habeas Corpus. It nonetheless existed, because it had been created by parliamentary history and by court decisions interpreting the common law. The men of Massachusetts wrote to Lord Chatham in 1768 that, "That grand principle in Nature, 'that what a man hath honestly acquired is absolutely and uncontrollably his own,' is established as a fundamental rule in the British Constitution."

The Americans also inherited the English parliamentary conspiracy theory: the belief, held first by the Puritans and later by the Whigs, that the crown or the executive periodically sought to subvert the British Constitution and turn the realm into a tyranny. The Americans believed that they themselves were the victims of such an assault in the 1770s. This was probably the biggest single influence upon the Constitution. For guidance in meeting this threat, they looked not so much forward to the French-style utopia as backward to the English civil war of the 1640s, and in particular to the great compilation of documents concerning it, edited by John Rushworth. As Jefferson put it, "What we did was with the help of Rushworth, whom we rummaged over for revolutionary precedents of those days." If we omit its beginning and end, the Declaration of Independence is essentially an old-style English parliamentary remonstrance, a collection of grievances seeking to justify armed opposition to authority, of a type going back to the thirteenth century. To my mind it is likewise significant that the Constitution begins with the legislative (i.e. the parliamentary) power and only then goes on to the executive. Its underlying aim is similar to those of the Whigs in England: to create a presidency which is, in effect, a circumscribed crown, a constitutional monarchy. What they sought was the old English objective: a limited government, with no standing army and low taxes, placed firmly under the law. Its joint custodians were the elected representatives of the people and judges with absolute security of tenure "during good behavior." In short, the Americans were really putting the British Constitution (as they saw it) in writing, but improving it by making the separation of powers formal and by adapting it to their own needs.

There was a third element, perhaps as important as the common law tradition, and equally organic—what I call the biblical spirit. Early America was a society saturated in the Bible and in the constitutional lesson that the Bible taught, especially in its popular historical books, Samuel and Kings. This lesson underwrote Whig conspiracy theory: It taught that kings or governments might be necessary, but that they had a natural propensity to evil and had to be curbed by prophets like Samuel, Elijah, and Elisha; in the Bible, God, through his prophets, forms the constitutional opposition to overweening executive power. The biblical spirit went even deeper, for it stressed that man is not merely a civic animal but also a moral one; his public acts—his politics— take place within an ethical, indeed, religious, framework. God is the primal legislator and the ultimate ratifying party of any constitution.

THE UNWRITTEN CONSTITUTION

We have to remember that the great document of 1787 was not the first American constitution: it was the first federal one. From the very beginning, American constitutional documents had a religious setting, usually explicit. The very first, drawn up by the Pilgrims on the Mayflower in 1620, was written "for the glory of God and the advancement of the Christian faith" and stated their desire "solemnly and mutually in the presence of God [to] covenant and combine ourselves together in a civil body politic." The first written constitution in the modern sense of the term, the Fundamental Orders of Connecticut (1639) asserted that the state owes its origin to "the wise disposition of the divine providence," the Bible requiring "an orderly and decent Government according to God, [to] maintain and preserve the liberty and purity of the Gospel." Massachusetts based its first New England law code (1641) on "humanity, civility and Christianity" and William Penn, framing his constitution for Pennsylvania in 1682, wrote, "Government seems to me a part of religion itself, a thing sacred in its institution."

All the early law codes and state constitutions accepted religion as the natural context of government. Indeed the emotional dynamic to the American Revolution was the first specifically American religious revival, the Great Awakening, which began in the 1730s. The first American widely known outside his own state, the first national figure, was not a politician but a preacher, George Whitefield. The Declaration of Independence itself invokes in its defense "the Laws of Nature and of Nature's God," and states that the right to "Life, Liberty and the Pursuit of Happiness" exists because men were so "endowed by their Creator." Hence the new society was placed under "the Protection of Divine Providence."

The Constitution itself was nonreligious because of the diversity of sects and the number of states, some of which guaranteed toleration. But the United States was not thereby a secular state; it might be more accurately described as a moral and ethical society without a state religion. John Adams himself wrote in 1818 that the Revolution had been brought about because ordinary Americans had undergone "a change in their religious sentiments of their duties and obligations." To his mind, Christianity was the unwritten constitution of the United States because its moral teaching (not its dogmas) gave America its ethical base:

"One great advantage of the Christian religion is that it brings the great principles of the law of nature and nations, love your neighbour as yourself, and do to others as you would that others do to you, to the knowledge, belief and veneration of the whole people. . . . The duties and rights of the man and the citizen are thus taught from early infancy."

George Washington was equally clear that the formal language of the Constitution had to be vivified by the religious spirit. He began his first inaugural address (1789) with a prayer that God, "who rules over the universe, who presides in the councils of nations," should bless the new government. He added that "every step" by which America had become a new nation had been "distinguished by some token of providential agency." When he finally relinquished office in 1796 he again appealed for divine help, and in a notable passage he insisted that "Religion and morality are indispensable supports [of] political prosperity." Virtue and morality, he argued, were the "necessary spring of popular government [and] reason and experience both forbid us to expect that national morality can prevail in exclusion of religious principle."

The American Constitution was thus the product not just of abstract ideology but of two living, historic traditions. Of course it could, and did, formally amend itself; and these amendments, from 1791 onwards, are of immense importance. But the rapidity with which the Constitution developed a life of its own and so underwent informal, organic changes in response to the growth of the nation itself was even more significant. This is the real key to its success.

A FLAWED DOCUMENT

There was one notable failure, wholly disregarded at the time, but which points a ghostly and reproachful finger at the constitutional framers now. Although they were preoccupied with civil rights, and many of the early amendments (one to eight, for example) are specifically designed to reinforce them, the doctrine of rights in the American Constitution excluded the Indians. The Declaration of Independence, in fact, treats them as enemies, accusing Britain of being in league with these "merciless Indian Savages," whose "known rule of warfare is an undistinguished destruction of all ages, sexes and conditions." And if the Constitution itself did nothing for the Indians, the second generation of rulers were, if anything, even more hostile to their interests. The Indian Treaties of 1814, 1816, 1817, 1818, and 1820, which were imposed by force and bribery rather than negotiation, were fatal to the long-term survival of the Indians, not least because they set the pattern for many more. The Indians had enjoyed more rights and security under the colonial system than under the republic, and even a man like John Quincy Adams, the sixth president, who was wholeheartedly on the side of Negro rights, had no sympathy whatever for America's original inhabitants. They were lucky, he wrote, to get any treaties at all; the alternative was "taking the lands for nothing, or exterminating the Indians." He argued that "to condemn vast regions of territory to perpetual barrenness and solitude that a few hundred savages might find wild beasts to hunt upon it [was] incompatible with the moral as well as the physical nature of things." This was the almost universal view for many decades.

With Negroes it was different: There, the organic element in the Constitution worked slowly but inexorably in their favor. The original document itself was, of course, a slave constitution, since ARTICLE I, SECTION 2, CLAUSE 3 allowed the slave states to count unfree persons, for representational purposes, as "three fifths of all other Persons," although slaves had no political rights whatever in any state constitution. The ironic but intended effect was to allow slave states to count their slaves in the political balance while denying them liberty. As late as 1800 only three states were slave-free. Thereafter, new states, whether slave or free, were admitted in such a way as to preserve the balance, the process being formalized in the Missouri Compromise of 1820. But this was only reached after long and furious debates and the balance was precarious right from the start. Indeed, precisely because the Constitution had an unwritten, moral dimension, even the slave-owning members of the Virginia dynasty, who largely created America, agreed that slavery posed a problem the country had to solve. Jefferson, the third president, thought it corrupted all of society since "the whole commerce between master and slave is a perpetual exercise of . . . the most unremitting despotism on the one part, and degrading submission on the other." James Madison, the fourth president, told Harriet Martineau, "With regard to slavery he owned himself almost to be in despair . . . acknowledging all the evils with which it has ever been charged." Both these men owned slaves. They admitted slavery had to go because otherwise America made no moral sense. But how to do it without breaking up the union?

John Quincy Adams, from the other side of the divide, was prepared to take the risk of breakup. "It is among the evils of slavery," he wrote in 1820, "that it taints the very sources of moral principle"; its elimination was therefore essential to America's constitutional health: "If the Union must be dissolved, slavery is precisely the question upon which it ought to break!" By reaching the compromise of 1820, Congress did not resolve the controversy or even put it to sleep; it merely postponed a violent solution. This was probably wise, for if the slavery issue had been pressed in 1820 the union would have broken up, whereas by the 1860s it was strong enough to survive even civil war. One of the lessons of American history is that there are times when it is right to compromise even on the most fundamental issues, political and moral; the spirit of the Constitution made such judicious delays possible.

BROADENING DEMOCRACY

Where the Constitution's organic nature proved most valuable was the almost effortless way in which it allowed the second and third generation of Americans to alter the fundamental nature of their government, changing it from an oligarchy to a democracy. Jefferson conceived America as a virtuous republic run by a rural elite whose rustic roots in their estates would protect them from urban vice. The Constitution was framed to provide indirect election by colleges of prominent citizens. Washington would have been horrified by the notion of a president elected directly by universal suffrage organized on party lines. He devoted the central core of his Farewell Address to a warning against the growth of party. He feared, first and foremost, that parties would emerge with a geographical basis and physically tear the union apart; but he also thought it right to "take a more comprehensive view" and warn Congress "in the most solemn manner against the baneful effects of the Spirit of Party, generally." Parties did in fact form and re-form, but until the mid-1820s there was a prevailing view that the administration should be above party. Monroe tried to make his cabinet representative of every major point of view, and John Quincy Adams deliberately refrained from firing his cabinet opponents for just this reason. Rule by an elite consensus remained the ideal and to some extent the practice.

But America was changing too fast to make the original constitutional position tenable. Before he died, fifty years after the Declaration, Jefferson was obliged to admit that virtue might be found in the burgeoning American cities too; indeed, the new prevailing orthodoxy, set down by George Tucker, was that the city was the source of progress. That in itself meant democracy in the long run. But in any case, the suffrage was in the hands of state legislatures and they were under constant pressure to extend it. Only Vermont had always had universal male voting; the rest originally had heavy property or tax qualifications and all voted for the president indirectly. But the system of indirect voting was discredited at the election of 1824; General Jackson got the largest number of suffrages and electoral college votes but the decision went (under the Constitution) to the House, where it was decided in favor of John Quincy Adams by what Jackson argued was a "corrupt bargain." Even by that date, only six states had kept the original method for electing a president.

The rest were switching to direct voting and extending the suffrage, too. By 1830 Maine had joined Vermont in adopting universal male suffrage, while seven other states gave it to all white males. Nine demanded mere tax qualifications. Only five kept property qualifications substantial. Jackson's men were able to organize his 1828 campaign on almost modern party lines through a federation of local machines, and he won because America was already virtually a democracy. As president he reinforced the trend of party rule by the spoils system, and by introducing a kitchen cabinet. By the mid-1830s he had virtually created the modern presidency, something quite different from the one envisaged in the Constitution.

The states themselves were thus chiefly responsible for expanding the democratic element. By 1834, when George Bancroft, America's first great historian, published the opening volume of the *History of the United States*, the democratic principle had become ideology. The constitutional movement towards democracy, he wrote, was the work of a "favoring providence"; the common man was the source both of freedom and happiness: "The best government rests on the people, not on the few, on persons, not on property."

Yet there were others who felt that a union that merely counted heads and ignored the practical power of wealth and property simply would not work. This was where the judicial arm came in as a balancing factor. John Marshall, the first great chief justice, was sceptical of the capacity of most men to govern themselves. He associated democracy with disorder, and both with state legislatures. He came from the conservative common law tradition of the English judiciary and he interpreted the Constitution as English judges used the common law, to advance practical, commonsense morality. His court, in a series of key decisions (Fletcher v Peck [1810]; Sturges v Crowninshield [1819]; McCulloch v Maryland [1819], etc.) countered the disorderly and destructive tendency of democracy (as he saw it) by reinforcing the federal, as opposed to state, constitution and by upholding the rights of property and particularly the sanctity of contracts.

Both Jacksonian democracy and Marshall's legal philosophy appealed to the essence of the Constitution and the religious morality that underlay it. The Jacksonians claimed they were "rescuing" the Constitution from an arrogant oligarchy, Marshall that he was protecting it from the ravages of a propertyless mob. In fact both were transforming it. Jackson was turning it into a presidential democracy; Marshall was making America safe for capitalism. Both were performing necessary and complementary functions. Without universal suffrage and direct election on the one hand, America could not have accommodated the greatest and most productive migration the world has ever known. Without a legal structure that protected property rights, America could not have developed its immense resources and pursued its manifest destiny to the Pacific. Democracy and capitalism each curbed the excesses of the other, and both merged eventually to produce the democratic capitalism that is the essential ideology of America in the last phase of the twentieth century. Each is rooted in the Constitution; each emerged from it by a natural process of organic growth. As Marshall himself put it in Gibbons v Ogden, "We must never forget that it is a constitution we are expounding, . . . something organic, capable of growth, susceptible to change."

It is because the U.S. Constitution possessed this merit from the start that it survived. And because, after two hundred years, it retains this natural capacity for growth, it seems likely to endure for as long as we can foresee.

Historian Paul Johnson is the author of 28 books, including the much-acclaimed Modern Times: The World from the 1920s to the 1990s.

CRITICAL THINKING QUESTIONS

1. How does the author define "constitutionalism"?
2. What does the content and stability of a constitution indicate about the country it serves?
3. How did the Enlightenment influence the writers of the Constitution?
4. What does the author mean when he describes the early United States as a "a moral and ethical society without a state religion"?
5. How did the Constitution fail Native Americans?

3

Federalism

A Fickle Federalism:
The Rehnquist Court Hobbles
Congress—and the States, Too

Richard Briffault

The revival of a doctrine of federalism that constrains the power of Congress has been a signature feature of the work of the Rehnquist Court. The Court's five-justice conservative majority has repeatedly held that the preservation of states' rights re quires broad new limits on what the national government may do to protect its citizens. Indeed, the Court has invalidated a number of federal laws on these grounds, including part of the Violence Against Women Act, the background-check provision of the Brady Handgun Violence Protection Act and provisions giving individuals the right to sue state governments for violating the Fair Labor Standards Act, the Age Discrimination in Employment Act and the Americans with Disabilities Act.

The Rehnquist Court's jurisprudence in this area has had a strained and curious quality. Although the five conservative justices claim to be strict constructionists, their federalism decisions are not rooted in the text of the Constitution. Nor are they particularly attentive to the values at the core of the federalist model of government: respect for interstate diversity, political experimentation and grass-roots participation. Instead, these decisions are extremely formalistic, taking state power as an end in itself rather than a means for promoting the rights and interests of the people.

Reprinted with permission from Richard Briffault, "A Fickle Federalism," *The American Prospect*, Volume 14, Number 3: March 01, 2003. The American Prospect, 11 Beacon Street, Suite 1120, Boston, MA 02108. All rights reserved.

At the same time, the broader body of the Court's work displays an inconsistent interest in empowering the states. Most famously in *Bush v. Gore* but also in a variety of cases challenging state regulation of such things as cigarette advertising and HMOs, most of the justices who in other settings support states' rights have sought to curtail state powers, cut off state initiatives and limit the states' ability to vindicate political rights. Rather than demonstrating a principled commitment to the autonomy of the states, the justices' opinions shift with the context—leaving the Court open to the charge that, like many politicians, it is using states' rights as a doctrinal rallying cry for other political ends.

THE COURT'S CONSERVATIVE MAJORITY HAS MOVED along three paths to limit the power of the federal government. First, the Court has been restricting the subjects on which Congress can legislate. Second, it has prohibited Congress from requiring state and local governments to help enforce national laws. And third, it has denied individual citizens the ability to sue states that violate national laws.

The shrinking of Congress' range of action has been startling. For six decades beginning in the 1930s, the Court had held that the Constitution's grant of authority to Congress to regulate "commerce . . . among the several states" provided the basis for a wide variety of economic and social legislation. But in 1995, in *United States v. Lopez,* the Rehnquist Court began to turn that around. Lopez invalidated the Gun-Free School Zones Act of 1990, which had made it a federal crime to possess a firearm within a certain distance of a school. To reach this decision, the five-justice majority asserted the traditional primacy of the states with respect to law enforcement and education—although the Constitution neither assigns these issues to the states nor places them beyond the scope of national power. The Court majority also claimed that there was no demonstrated connection between guns in schools and economic activity (commerce).

Lopez initially seemed an isolated decision. Many observers assumed that if Congress made a greater effort in the future to show the economic impact of a problem and the need for national legislation to address it, the Court would return to its longstanding acceptance of Congress' authority, under the commerce clause, to act on matters of national importance.

That reading of Lopez, however, was exploded in 2000 in *United States v. Morrison,* when the Court invalidated the part of the Violence Against Women Act that provided a federal civil remedy for victims of gender-motivated violence. Before passing this law, Congress held hearings and made extensive findings concerning the economic costs of gender-based violence and the history of state inaction that made it necessary for the federal government to do something. The five-justice majority, however, ruled that even though gender violence actually affects commerce, it is essentially a noncommercial concern and, thus, beyond Congress' power to regulate. The line Morrison attempts to draw between commercial and noncommercial concerns recalls the Court's fruitless struggle nearly a century ago to limit the reach of the commerce clause by creating a standard that would distinguish interstate from intrastate economic activity. The commercial-noncommercial distinction is inherently just as murky, subjective and open to manipulation. Moreover, many noncommercial matters—civil rights, protection of endangered species, education, criminal law—have implications for the entire country, which Congress needs to be able to address.

The potential threat to environmental regulation was underscored in a 2001 case in which the Court narrowed the range of "navigable waters" protected by the Clean Water Act, thereby allowing a municipal solid-waste disposal site to open without a federal permit. Although this case turned on statutory interpretation rather than the Constitution, Chief Justice William Rehnquist, writing for the majority, emphasized that the case involved "the outer limits of Congress' power," hinting that there may be constitutional limits on the federal government's authority to protect the environment.

THE COURT'S SECOND LINE OF FEDERALISM cases rests on its determination that the 10th Amendment prohibits the federal government from requiring states and local governments to help implement federal programs. In fact, the 10th Amendment says little more than that powers not granted to the federal government or denied to the states are reserved to the states, but the Court interpreted this as invalidating part of the Brady bill. In 1997, without questioning Congress' power to regulate gun purchases, the Court held that the provision of the Brady act that required local law-enforcement officers to conduct background checks on prospective gun buyers unconstitutionally "commandeered" administrative support.

The five justices who advanced the so-called anti-commandeering doctrine contend that federalism would be better served, and the states' interests better protected, if the national government were to take over a field—that is, create a new federal bureaucracy and entirely displace state laws and officers— rather than rely on local officials to enforce its rules. But nothing in the text of the Constitution requires this. Nor is such a policy necessary to protect the autonomy of the states in a federal system. The European Union, in fact, has reached exactly the opposite conclusion, deciding that its member states are best served if the federal government is required to turn to them to carry out its policies. It is difficult to see how states here would be better protected by a rule that could lead, for example, to the creation of a national police force responsible for local law enforcement.

THE COURT'S THIRD FEDERALISM INITIATIVE—ITS dramatic expansion of the states' "sovereign immunity" from citizen lawsuits—is the most at odds with traditional notions of federalism as a mechanism for promoting liberty by diffusing power. These cases grow out of the 11th Amendment, which bars a citizen of one state from suing another state in federal court. More than a century ago, the Supreme Court interpreted this amendment broadly to also apply to citizens suing their own states. In modern times, the scope of the amendment has been sharply contested, with the Court holding that Congress can abrogate state sovereign immunity when it passes laws under the commerce clause or to enforce the due-process and equal-protection provisions of the 14th Amendment. Under those decisions, Congress could authorize individuals to sue a state for damages should the state government violate rights created by federal law.

In 1996, however, the Rehnquist Court, in a 5-to-4 decision, shifted gears and ruled that Congress cannot subject a state to private lawsuits even as part of a legitimate program of domestic regulation under the commerce clause. Since then, the Court has ruled that people cannot sue a state that violates their rights under federal minimum wage laws, laws protecting older and disabled workers, and patent laws.

Indeed, the Court has gone well beyond the 11th Amendment, which speaks only of suits in federal court. In 1999 the Court also barred citizens from suing in state court to enforce federal rights. And in 2002 the Court extended sovereign immunity to a federal administrative proceeding. In that instance, the Court candidly abandoned the idea that the states' immunity is rooted in the text of the Constitution and cited instead the fundamental importance of protecting the states' "dignity."

To be sure, certain individual claims may still be brought against a state. Those based on the 14th Amendment are allowed—although the Court has narrowed Congress' power to protect 14th Amendment rights. In addition, the Court has held that the states' sovereign immunity does not bar the federal government itself from suing them. But here again, as in the anti-commandeering doctrine, the Court seems to be saying that federalism and state autonomy would be better served by a greater federal intervention than by a lesser. The Court suggests that a massive federal bureaucratic enforcement effort against the states would be preferable to allowing individuals to vindicate their own rights directly. This is entirely inconsistent with the notion of federalism as a curb on big government. Furthermore, in an era of budget deficits, Congress is not likely to dramatically increase the resources given to federal agencies so they can enforce laws that are no longer subject to private enforcement actions. A cynic might say that allowing only federal agencies to enforce these laws is simply a guarantee of underenforcement.

The sovereign immunity cases epitomize the worst of the Court's formalistic federalism. Invoking a doctrine from the era of King George III, these cases lay out a vision of the states as separate from, hostile to and ultimately above their own people. Going well beyond the limited language of the 11th Amendment, they strike at the heart of the American belief that in our democracy, sovereignty is vested in the people, not the government.

INDEED, THE COURT'S FEDERALISM CASES SUGGEST AN indifference to the states' potential to act as democratic, locally accountable policy makers within our federal structure. And this impression is bolstered by other cases in which the Court has given the states short shrift. In the most obvious example—the Florida 2000 presidential recount—the Court dramatically intervened in an area traditionally left to the states, rejected the efforts of a state supreme court to provide more vigorous protection of the rights of Florida voters whose ballots had not been tabulated by local ballot-counting machinery, and opened the door to nationalization of election administration. Led by the Rehnquist bloc, the Court twice overturned the state supreme court's actions with little apparent concern about the implications for federalism.

In other settings, too, this group of justices has attached little weight to the value of enabling states to make policy decisions concerning matters important to their citizens. In *Lorillard Tobacco v. Reilly,* for instance, the Court invalidated Massachusetts regulations that sought to address the problem of youth smoking. Massachusetts had prohibited outdoor cigarette advertising near schools, public parks and playgrounds, and it had required point-of-sale advertising near those places to be more than five feet from the floor (and thus out of the reach of young children). The tobacco industry claimed that the Massachusetts rules were preempted by the federal cigarette labeling law, which requires a surgeon general's warning on cigarette packs and bars additional state regulation of cigarette advertising. Lower courts in this and several other cases had held that the federal law preempted only state regulation of the content and not the location of cigarette advertising. But in an opinion joined only by the five proponents of the new judicial federalism, the Supreme Court agreed with the industry that the limited, ambiguous language of the federal law entirely barred all state initiatives concerning cigarette advertising.

Similarly, in *Rush Prudential HMO v. Moran,* an HMO claimed that an Illinois law providing for an independent medical review of certain denials of benefits by HMOs was preempted by the Employee Retirement Income Security Act (ERISA), the federal law regulating employee pension and health benefits. ERISA generally displaces state laws regulating employee benefit plans. However, the Illinois law was not at odds with any specific provision of ERISA, which does not address HMOs at all. Moreover, ERISA provides that state laws regulating insurance are exempt from preemption. Nonetheless, the Court divided over the issue. Four of the five justices who support states' rights in the commerce clause, 10th Amendment and sovereign immunity settings concluded that the Illinois HMO law was preempted by ERISA. Though the Illinois law has counterparts in 40 other states, the four dismissed concerns about the impact that such a decision would have on the states' ability to develop policy in an area of vital importance to their residents. Only Justice Sandra Day O'Connor's defection from the bloc saved the Illinois statute.

As the preemption cases indicate, the Court's commitment to federalism is highly erratic. The Court's conservative majority may use a states' rights argument to strike down national actions, but the same justices may also be unsympathetic to state autonomy if it results in new state initiatives. Justice Louis Brandeis famously observed that states can be "laboratories of democracy," experimenting with new policies and providing for grass-roots participation. But you wouldn't know it from the Court's federalism jurisprudence.

Among politicians, the federalism issue does not cut cleanly between liberals and conservatives. Liberals who are normally states' rights skeptics are likely to support state measures regulating HMOs or cigarette advertising. Conservatives who celebrate states' rights will often try to expand federal power and burden the states when it suits their other interests. President Bush, for instance, contends that he is a strong proponent of state autonomy, but the cornerstone of his domestic agenda has been the No Child Left Behind Act, which extends federal regulation deep into the traditionally state-controlled area of primary and secondary education. Similarly, the president's small-pox vaccination program has effectively "commandeered" the resources of state and local public-health offices.

Constitutional law is supposed to be the domain of principle, not politics. But the justices of the Rehnquist bloc have been no more successful than politicians at making a principled commitment to a consistent doctrine of federalism. And the Court's essentially negative approach to the subject reflects little interest in or support for the positive policy-making role the states can play in our federal system.

Richard Briffault is the vice dean and Joseph P. Chamberlain Professor of Legislation at Columbia University Law School.

CRITICAL THINKING QUESTIONS

1. In what ways has the Rehnquist Court constrained the powers of Congress?
2. In what ways has the Rehnquist Court constrained the powers of the states?
3. How did the conservative majority on the Rehnquist Court reverse traditional powers of states by its 2000 ruling handing the presidency to George W. Bush?

4

Civil Liberties

Rights, Liberties, and Security: Recalibrating the Balance After September 11

Stuart Taylor, Jr.

W hen dangers increase, liberties shrink. That has been our history, especially in wartime. And today we face dangers without precedent: a mass movement of militant Islamic terrorists who crave martyrdom, hide in shadows, are fanatically bent on slaughtering as many of us as possible and—if they can—using nuclear truck bombs to obliterate New York or Washington or both, without leaving a clue as to the source of the attack.

How can we avert catastrophe and hold down the number of lesser mass murders?

Our best hope is to prevent al-Qaida from getting nuclear, biological, or chemical weapons and smuggling them into this country. But we need be unlucky only once to fail in that. Ultimately we can hold down our casualties only by finding and locking up (or killing) as many as possible of the hundreds or thousands of possible al-Qaida terrorists whose strategy is to infiltrate our society and avoid attention until they strike.

The urgency of penetrating secret terrorist cells makes it imperative for Congress—and the nation—to undertake a candid, searching, and systematic reassessment of the civil liberties rules that restrict the government's core investigative and detention powers. Robust national debate and deliberate congressional action should replace what has so far been largely ad hoc

Brookings Review, Wntr 2003, v21, i1, p25(7).

© 2003 Brookings Institution. Reprinted with permission.

presidential improvisation. While the USA-PATRIOT Act—no model of careful deliberation—changed many rules for the better (and some for the worse), it did not touch some others that should be changed.

Carefully crafted new legislation would be good not only for security but also for liberty. Stubborn adherence to the civil liberties status quo would probably damage our most fundamental freedoms far more in the long run than would judicious modifications of rules that are less fundamental. Considered congressional action based on open national debate is more likely to be sensitive to civil liberties and to the Constitution's checks and balances than unilateral expansion of executive power. Courts are more likely to check executive excesses if Congress sets limits for them to enforce. Government agents are more likely to respect civil liberties if freed from rules that create unwarranted obstacles to doing their jobs. And preventing terrorist mass murders is the best way of avoiding a panicky stampede into truly oppressive police statism, in which measures now unthinkable could suddenly become unstoppable.

This is not to advocate truly radical revisions of civil liberties. Nor is it to applaud all the revisions that have already been made, some of which seem unwarranted and even dangerous. But unlike most in-depth commentaries on the liberty-security balance since September 11—which argue (plausibly, on some issues) that we have gone too far in expanding government power—this article contends that in important respects we have not gone far enough. Civil libertarians have underestimated the need for broader investigative powers and exaggerated the dangers to our fundamental liberties. Judicious expansion of the government's powers to find suspected terrorists would be less dangerous to freedom than either risking possibly preventable attacks or resorting to incarceration without due process of law—as the Bush administration has begun to do. We should worry less about being wiretapped or searched or spied upon or interrogated and more about seeing innocent people put behind bars—or being blown to bits.

RECALIBRATING THE LIBERTY-SECURITY BALANCE

The courts, Congress, the president, and the public have from the beginning of this nation's history demarcated the scope of protected rights "by a weighing of competing interests . . . the public-safety interest and the liberty interest," in the words of Judge Richard A. Posner of the U.S. Court of Appeals for the Seventh Circuit. "The safer the nation feels, the more weight judges will be willing to give to the liberty interest."

During the 1960s and 1970s, the weight on the public safety side of the scales seemed relatively modest. The isolated acts of violence by groups like the Weather Underground and the Black Panthers—which had largely run their course by the mid-1970s—were a minor threat compared with our enemies today. Suicide bombers were virtually unheard of. By contrast, the threat to civil liberties posed by broad governmental investigative and detention powers and an imperial presidency had been dramatized by Watergate and by disclosures of such ugly abuses of power as FBI Director J. Edgar Hoover's spying on politicians, his wiretapping and harassment of the Reverend Martin Luther King, Jr., and the government's disruption and harassment of anti-war and radical groups.

To curb such abuses, the Supreme Court, Congress, and the Ford and Carter administrations placed tight limits on law-enforcement and intelligence agencies. The Court consolidated and in some ways extended the Warren Court's revolutionary restrictions on government powers to search, seize, wiretap, interrogate, and detain suspected criminals (and terrorists). It also barred warrantless wiretaps and searches of domestic radicals. Congress barred warrantless wiretaps and searches of suspected foreign spies and terrorists—a previously untrammeled presidential power—in the 1978 Foreign Intelligence Surveillance Act. And Edward Levi, President Ford's attorney general, clamped down on domestic surveillance by the FBI.

As a result, today many of the investigative powers that government could use to penetrate al-Qaida cells—surveillance, informants, searches, seizures, wiretaps, arrests, interrogations, detentions—are tightly restricted by a web of laws, judicial precedents, and administrative rules. Stalked in our homeland by the deadliest terrorists in history, we are armed with investigative powers calibrated largely for dealing with drug dealers, bank robbers, burglars, and ordinary murderers. We are also stuck in habits of mind that have not yet fully processed how dangerous our world has become or how ill-prepared our legal regime is to meet the new dangers.

RETHINKING GOVERNMENT'S POWERS

Only a handful of the standard law-enforcement investigative techniques have much chance of penetrating and defanging groups like al-Qaida. The four most promising are: infiltrating them through informants and undercover agents; finding them and learning their plans through surveillance, searches, and wiretapping; detaining them before they can launch terrorist attacks; and interrogating those detained. All but the first (infiltration) are now so tightly restricted by Supreme Court precedents (sometimes by mistaken or debatable readings of them), statutes, and administrative rules as to seriously impede terrorism investigators. Careful new legislation could make these powers more flexible and useful while simultaneously setting boundaries to minimize overuse and abuse.

SEARCHES AND SURVEILLANCE

The Supreme Court's case law involving the Fourth Amendment's ban on "unreasonable searches and seizures" does not distinguish clearly between a routine search for stolen goods or marijuana and a preventive search for a bomb or a vial of anthrax. To search a dwelling, obtain a wiretap, or do a thorough search of a car or truck, the government must generally have "probable cause"—often (if incorrectly) interpreted in the more-probable-than-not sense—to believe that the proposed search will uncover evidence of crime. These rules make little sense when the purpose of the search is to prevent mass murder.

Federal agents and local police alike need more specific guidance than the Supreme Court can quickly supply. Congress should provide it, in the form of legislation relaxing for terrorism investigations the restrictions on searching, seizing, and wiretapping, including the undue stringency of the burden of proof to obtain a search warrant in a terrorism investigation.

Search and seizure restrictions were the main (if widely unrecognized) cause of the FBI's famous failure to seek a warrant during the weeks before September 11 to search the computer and other possessions of Zacarias Moussaoui, the alleged "20th hijacker." He had been locked up since August 16, technically for overstaying his visa, based on a tip about his strange behavior at a Minnesota flight school. The FBI had ample reason to suspect that Moussaoui—who has since admitted to being a member of al-Qaida—was a dangerous Islamic militant plotting airline terrorism.

Congressional and journalistic investigations of the Moussaoui episode have focused on the intelligence agencies' failure to put together the Moussaoui evidence with other intelligence reports that should have alerted them that a broad plot to hijack airliners might be afoot. Investigators have virtually ignored the undue stringency of the legal restraints on the government's powers to investigate suspected terrorists. Until these are fixed, they will seriously hobble our intelligence agencies no matter how smart they are.

From the time of FDR until 1978, the government could have searched Moussaoui's possessions without judicial permission, by invoking the president's inherent power to collect intelligence about foreign enemies. But the 1978 Foreign Intelligence Security Act (FISA) bars searches of suspected foreign spies and terrorists unless the attorney general can obtain a warrant from a special national security court (the FISA court). The warrant application has to show not only that the target is a foreign terrorist, but also that he is a member of some international terrorist "group."

Coleen Rowley, a lawyer in the FBI's Minneapolis office, argued passionately in a widely publicized letter last May 21 to FBI Director Robert S. Mueller III that the information about Moussaoui satisfied this FISA requirement. Congressional investigators have said the same. FBI headquarters officials have disagreed, because before September 11 no evidence linked Moussaoui to al-Qaida or any other identifiable terrorist group. Unlike their critics, the FBI headquarters officials were privy to any relevant prior decisions by the FISA court, which cloaks its proceedings and decisions in secrecy. In addition, they were understandably gun-shy about going forward with a legally shaky warrant application in the wake of the FISA court's excoriation of an FBI supervisor in the fall of 2000 for perceived improprieties in his warrant applications. In any event, even if the FBI had done everything right, it is at least debatable whether its information about Moussaoui was sufficient to support a FISA warrant.

More important for future cases, it is clear that FISA—even as amended by the USA-PATRIOT Act—will not authorize a warrant in any case in which the FBI cannot tie a suspected foreign terrorist to one or more confederates, whether because his confederates have escaped detection or cannot be identified or because the suspect is a lone wolf.

Congress could strengthen the hand of FBI terrorism investigators by amending FISA to include the commonsense presumption that any foreign terrorist who comes to the United States is probably acting for (or at least inspired by) some international terrorist group. Another option would be to lower the burden of proof from "probable cause" to "reasonable suspicion." A third option—which could be extended to domestic as well as international terrorism investigations—would be to authorize a warrantless "preventive" search or wiretap of anyone the government has reasonable grounds to suspect of preparing or helping others prepare for a terrorist attack. To minimize any temptation for government agents to use this new power in pursuit of ordinary criminal suspects, Congress could prohibit the use in any prosecution unrelated to terrorism of any evidence obtained by such a preventive search or wiretap.

The Supreme Court seems likely to uphold any such statute as consistent with the ban on "unreasonable searches and seizures." While the Fourth Amendment says that "no warrants shall issue, but upon probable cause," warrants are not required for many types of searches, are issued for administrative searches of commercial property without probable cause in the traditional sense, and arguably should never be required. Even in the absence of a warrant or probable cause, the justices have upheld searches based on "reasonable suspicion" of criminal activities, including brief "stop-and-frisk" encounters on the streets and car stops. They have also upheld mandatory drug-testing of certain government employees and transportation workers whose work affects the public safety even when there is no particularized suspicion at all. In the latter two cases, the Court suggested that searches designed to prevent harm to the public safety should be easier to justify than searches seeking evidence for criminal cases.

EXAGGERATED FEAR OF BIG BROTHER

Proposals to increase the government's wiretapping powers awaken fears of unleashing Orwellian thought police to spy on, harass, blackmail, and smear political dissenters and others. Libertarians point out that most conversations overheard and e-mails intercepted in the war on terrorism will be innocent and that the tappers and buggers will over-hear intimacies and embarrassing disclosures that are none of the government's business.

Such concerns argue for taking care to broaden wiretapping and surveillance powers only as much as seems reasonable to prevent terrorist acts. But broader wiretapping authority is not all bad for civil liberties. It is a more accurate and benign method of penetrating terrorist cells than the main alternative, which is planting and recruiting informers—a dangerous, ugly, and unreliable business in which the government is already free to engage without limit. The narrower the government's surveillance powers, the more it will rely on informants.

Moreover, curbing the government's power to collect information through wiretapping is not the only way to protect against misuse of the information. Numerous other safeguards less damaging to the counterterrorism effort—inspectors general, the Justice Department's Office of Professional Responsibility, congressional investigators, a gaggle of liberal and conservative civil liberties groups, and the news media—have become extremely potent. The FBI has very little incentive to waste time and resources on unwarranted snooping.

To keep the specter of Big Brother in perspective, it's worth recalling that the president had unlimited power to wiretap suspected foreign spies and terrorists until 1978 (when FISA was adopted); if this devastated privacy or liberty, hardly anyone noticed. It's also worth noting that despite the government's already-vast power to comb through computerized records of our banking and commercial transactions and much else that we do in the computer age, the vast majority of the people who have seen their privacy or reputations shredded have not been wronged by rogue officials. They have been wronged by media organizations, which do far greater damage to far, more people with far less accountability.

Nineteen years ago, in *The Rise of the Computer State*, David Burnham wrote: "The question looms before us: Can the United States continue to flourish and grow in an age when the physical movements, individual purchases, conversations and meetings of every citizen are constantly under surveillance by private companies and government agencies?" It can. It has. And now that the computer state has risen indeed, the threat of being watched by Big Brother or smeared by the FBI seems a lot smaller than the threat of being blown to bits or poisoned by terrorists.

THE CASE FOR COERCIVE INTERROGATION

The same Zacarias Moussaoui whose possessions would have been searched but for FISA'S undue stringency also epitomizes another problem: the perverse impact of the rules—or what are widely assumed to be the rules—restricting interrogations of suspected terrorists.

"We were prevented from even attempting to question Moussaoui on the day of the attacks when, in theory, he could have possessed further information about other co-conspirators," Coleen Rowley complained in a little-noticed portion of her May 21 letter to Mueller. The reason was that Moussaoui had requested a lawyer. To the FBI that meant that any further interrogation would violate the Fifth Amendment "Miranda rules" laid down by the Supreme Court in 1966 and subsequent cases.

It's not hard to imagine such rules (or such an interpretation) leading to the loss of countless lives. While interrogating Moussaoui on September 11 might not have yielded any useful information, suppose that he had been part of a team planning a second wave of hijackings later in September and that his resistance could have been cracked. Or suppose that the FBI learns tomorrow, from a wiretap, that another al-Qaida team is planning an imminent attack and arrests an occupant of the wiretapped apartment.

We all know the drill. Before asking any questions, FBI agents (and police) must warn the suspect: "You have a right to remain silent." And if the suspect asks for a lawyer, all interrogation must cease until the lawyer arrives (and tells the suspect to keep quiet). This seems impossible to justify when dealing with people suspected of planning mass murder. But it's the law, isn't it?

Actually, it's not the law, though many judges think it is, along with most lawyers, federal agents, police, and cop-show mavens. You do not have a right to remain silent. The most persuasive interpretation of the Constitution and the Supreme Court's precedents is that agents and police are free to interrogate any suspect without Miranda warnings; to spurn requests for a lawyer; to press hard for answers; and—at least in a terrorism investigation—perhaps even to use hours of interrogation, verbal abuse, isolation, blindfolds, polygraph tests, death-penalty threats, and other forms of psychological coercion short of torture or physical brutality. Maybe even truth serum.

The Fifth Amendment self-incrimination clause says only that no person "shall be compelled in any criminal case to be a witness against himself." The clause prohibits forcing a defendant to testify at his trial and also making him a witness against himself indirectly by using compelled pretrial statements. It does not prohibit compelling a suspect to talk. Miranda held only that in determining whether a defendant's statements (and information derived from them) may be used against him at his trial, courts must treat all interrogations of arrested suspects as inherently coercive unless the warnings are given.

Courts typically ignore this distinction because in almost every litigated case the issue is whether a criminal defendant's incriminating statements should be suppressed at his trial; there is no need to focus on whether the constitutional problem is the conduct of the interrogation, or the use at trial of evidence obtained, or both. And as a matter of verbal shorthand, it's a lot easier to say "the police violated Miranda" than to say "the judge would be violating Miranda if he or she were to admit the defendant's statements into evidence at his trial."

But the war against terrorism has suddenly increased the significance of this previously academic question. In terrorism investigations, it will often be more important to get potentially life-saving information from a suspect than to get incriminating statements for use in court.

Fortunately for terrorism investigators, the Supreme Court said in 1990 that "a constitutional violation [of the Fifth Amendment's self-incrimination clause] occurs only at trial." It cited an earlier ruling that the government can obtain court orders compelling reluctant witnesses to talk and can imprison them for contempt of court if they refuse, if it first guarantees them immunity from prosecution on the basis of their statements or any derivative evidence. These decisions support the conclusion that the self-incrimination clause "does not forbid the forcible extraction of information but only the use of information so extracted as evidence in a criminal case," as a federal appeals court ruled in 1992.

Of course, even when the primary reason for questioning a suspected terrorist is prevention, the government could pay a heavy cost for ignoring

Miranda and using coercive interrogation techniques, because it would sometimes find it difficult or impossible to prosecute extremely dangerous terrorists. But terrorism investigators may be able to get their evidence and use it too, if the Court—or Congress, which unlike the Court would not have to wait for a proper case to come along—extends a 1984 precedent creating what the justices called a "public safety" exception to Miranda. That decision allowed use at trial of a defendant's incriminating answer to a policeman's demand (before any Miranda warnings) to know where his gun was hidden.

Those facts are not a perfect parallel for most terrorism investigations, because of the immediate nature of the danger (an accomplice might pick up the gun) and the spontaneity of the officer's question. And as Rowley testified, "In order to give timely advice" about what an agent can legally do, "you've got to run to a computer and pull it up, and I think that many people have kind of forgotten that case, and many courts have actually limited it to its facts."

But when the main purpose of the interrogation is to prevent terrorist attacks, the magnitude of the danger argues for a broader public safety exception, as Rowley implied in her letter.

Congress should neither wait for the justices to clarify the law nor assume that they will reach the right conclusions without prodding. It should make the rules as clear as possible as soon as possible. Officials like Rowley need to know that they are free to interrogate suspected terrorists more aggressively than they suppose. While a law expanding the public safety exception to Miranda would be challenged as unconstitutional, it would contradict no existing Supreme Court precedent and—if carefully calibrated to apply only when the immediate purpose is to save lives—would probably be upheld.

Would investigators routinely ignore Miranda and engage in coercive interrogation—perhaps extorting false confessions—if told that the legal restraints were far looser than had been supposed? The risk would not be significantly greater than it is now. Police would still need to comply with Miranda in almost all cases for fear of jeopardizing any prosecution. While that would not be true in terrorism investigations if the public safety exception were broadened, extreme abuses such as beatings and torture would violate the due process clause of the Fifth Amendment (and of the Fourteenth Amendment as well), which has been construed as barring interrogation techniques that "shock the conscience," and is backed up by administrative penalties and the threat of civil lawsuits.

BRINGING PREVENTIVE DETENTION
INSIDE THE LAW

Of all the erosions of civil liberties that must be considered since September 11, preventive detention—incarcerating people because of their perceived dangerousness even when they are neither convicted nor charged with any crime—would represent the sharpest departure from centuries of Anglo-American jurisprudence and come closest to police statism.

But the case for some kind of preventive detention has never been as strong. Al-Qaida's capacity to inflict catastrophic carnage dwarfs any previous domestic security threat. Its "sleeper" agents are trained to avoid criminal activities that might arouse suspicion. So the careful ones cannot be arrested on criminal charges until it is too late. And their lust for martyrdom renders criminal punishment ineffective as a deterrent.

Without preventive detention, the Bush administration would apparently have no solid legal basis for holding the two U.S. citizens in military brigs in this country as suspected "enemy combatants"—or for holding the more than 500 noncitizens at Guantanamo Bay. Nor would it have had a solid legal basis for detaining any of the 19 September 11 hijackers if it had suspected them of links to al-Qaida before they struck. Nor could it legally have detained Moussaoui—who was suspected of terrorist intent but was implicated in no provable crime or conspiracy—had he had not overstayed his visa.

What should the government do when it is convinced of a suspect's terrorist intent but lacks admissible evidence of any crime? Or when a criminal trial would blow vital intelligence secrets? Or when ambiguous evidence makes it a tossup whether a suspect is harmless or an al-Qaidan? What should it do with suspects like Jose Padilla, who was arrested in Chicago and is now in military detention because he is suspected of (but not charged with) plotting a radioactive "dirty-bomb" attack on Washington, D.C.? Or with a (hypothetical) Pakistani graduate student in chemistry, otherwise unremarkable, who has downloaded articles about how terrorists might use small planes to start an anthrax epidemic and shown an intense but unexplained interest in crop-dusters?

Only four options exist. Let such suspects go about their business unmonitored until (perhaps) they commit mass murders; assign agents to tail them until (perhaps) they give the agents the slip; bring prosecutions without solid evidence and risk acquittals; and preventive detention. The last could theoretically include not only incarceration but milder restraints such as house arrest or restriction to certain areas combined with agreement to carry (or to be implanted with) a device enabling the government to track the suspect's movements at all times.

As an alternative to preventive detention, Congress could seek to facilitate prosecutions of suspected "sleepers" by allowing use of now-inadmissible and secret evidence and stretching the already broad concept of criminal conspiracy so far as to make it almost a thought crime. But that would have a harsher effect on innocent terrorism suspects than would preventive detention and could weaken protections for all criminal defendants.

As Alan Dershowitz notes, "[N]o civilized nation confronting serious danger has ever relied exclusively on criminal convictions for past offenses. Every country has introduced, by one means or another, a system of preventive or administrative detention for persons who are thought to be dangerous but who might not be convictable under the conventional criminal law."

The best argument against preventive detention of suspected international terrorists is history's warning that the system will be abused, could expand inexorably—especially in the panic that might follow future attacks—and has such terrifying potential for infecting the entire criminal justice system and undermining our Bill of Rights that we should never start down that road. What is terrorist intent, and how may it be proved? Through a suspect's advocacy of a terrorist group's cause? Association with its members or sympathizers? If preventive detention is okay for people suspected of (but not charged with) terrorist intent, what about people suspected of homicidal intent, or violent proclivities, or dealing drugs?

These are serious concerns. But the dangers of punishing dissident speech, guilt by association, and overuse of preventive detention could be controlled by careful legislation. This would not be the first exception to the general rule against preventive detention. The others have worked fairly well. They include pretrial detention without bail of criminal defendants found to be dangerous, civil commitment of people found dangerous by reason of mental illness, and medical quarantines, a practice that may once again be necessary in the event of bioterrorism. All in all, the danger that a preventive-detention regime for suspected terrorists would take us too far down the slippery slope toward police statism is simply not as bad as the danger of letting would-be mass murderers roam the country.

In any event, we already have a preventive-detention regime for suspected international terrorists—three regimes, in fact, all created and controlled by the Bush administration without congressional input. First, two U.S. citizens—Jose Padilla, the suspected would-be dirty bomber arrested in Chicago, and Yaser Esam Hamdi, a Louisiana-born Saudi Arabian captured in Afghanistan and taken first to Guantanamo—have been in military brigs in this country for many months without being charged with any crime or allowed to see any lawyer or any judge. The administration claims that it never has to prove anything to anyone. It says that even U.S. citizens arrested in this country—who may have far stronger grounds than battlefield detainees for denying that they are enemy combatants—are entitled to no due process whatever once the government puts that label on them. This argument is virtually unprecedented, wrong as a matter of law, and indefensible as a matter of policy.

Second, Attorney General John Ashcroft rounded up more than 1,100 mostly Muslim noncitizens in the fall of 2001, which involved preventive detention in many cases although they were charged with immigration violations or crimes (mostly minor) or held under the material witness statute. This when-in-doubt-detain approach effectively reversed the presumption of innocence in the hope of disrupting any planned follow-up attacks. We may never know whether it succeeded in this vital objective. But the legal and moral bases for holding hundreds of apparently harmless detainees, sometimes without access to legal counsel, in conditions of unprecedented secrecy, seemed less and less plausible as weeks and months went by. Worse, the administration treated many (if not most) of the detainees shabbily and some abusively. (By mid-2002, the vast majority had been deported or released.)

Third, the Pentagon has incarcerated hundreds of Arab and other prisoners captured in Afghanistan at Guantanamo, apparently to avoid the jurisdiction of all courts—and has refused to create a fair, credible process for determining which are in fact enemy combatants and which of those are "unlawful."

These three regimes have been implemented with little regard for the law, for the rights of the many (mostly former) detainees who are probably innocent, or for international opinion. It is time for Congress to step in—to authorize a regime of temporary preventive detention for suspected international terrorists, while circumscribing that regime and specifying strong safeguards against abuse.

CIVIL LIBERTIES FOR A NEW ERA

It is senseless to adhere to overly broad restrictions imposed by decades-old civil-liberties rules when confronting the threat of unprecedented carnage at the hands of modern terrorists. In the words of Harvard Law School's Laurence H. Tribe, "The old adage that it is better to free 100 guilty men than to imprison one innocent describes a calculus that our Constitution—which is no suicide pact—does not impose on government when the 100 who are freed belong to terrorist cells that slaughter innocent civilians, and may well have access to chemical, biological, or nuclear weapons." The question is not whether we should increase governmental power to meet such dangers. The question is how much.

Stuart Taylor, Jr., is a senior writer for National Journal.

CRITICAL THINKING QUESTIONS

1. What does the author say about the USA-Patriot Act?
2. Why did Congress place strict limits on the ability of government to conduct wiretaps, surveillance, etc. in the 1970s?
3. What are the author's proposals for both protecting civil liberties and allowing vigorous prosecution of the war on terrorism in America?
4. What are your opinions of the author's proposals?
5. How do you think the government should act to prevent further terrorist attacks in the United States?

5

Civil Rights

Affirmative Action: Don't Mend It or End It—Bend It

Peter H. Schuck

Affirmative action policy—by which I mean ethnoracial preferences in
the allocation of socially valuable resources—is even more divisive and
unsettled today than at its inception more than 30 years ago.

Affirmative action's policy context has changed dramatically since 1970.
One change is legal. Since the Supreme Court's 1978 Bakke decision, when
Justice Lewis Powell's pivotal fifth vote endorsed certain "diversity"-based
preferences in higher education, the Court has made it increasingly difficult
for affirmative action plans to pass constitutional muster unless they are carefully designed to remedy specific past acts of discrimination. Four other
changes the triumph of the nondiscrimination principle: blacks' large social
gains; evidence on the size, beneficiaries, and consequences of preferences:
and new demographic realities—persuade me that affirmative action as we
know it should be abandoned even if it is held to be constitutional.

"As we know it" is the essential qualifier in that sentence. I propose neither a wholesale ban on affirmative action ("ending" it) nor tweaks in its administration ("mending" it). Rather, I would make two structural changes to
curtail existing preferences while strengthening the remaining ones' claim to
justice. First, affirmative action would be banned in the public sector but allowed in the private sector. Second, private-sector institutions that use preferences would be required to disclose how and why they do so. These reforms
would allow the use of preferences by private institutions that believe in them

Brookings Review, Wntr 2002, v20, i1, p24(4).

© 2002 Brookings Institution. Reprinted with permission.

enough to disclose and defend them, while doing away with the obfuscation, duplicity, and lack of accountability that too often accompany preferences. Affirmative action could thus be localized and customized to suit the varying requirements of particular contexts and sponsors.

TRIUMPH OF THE NONDISCRIMINATION
PRINCIPLE

Why is change necessary? To explain, one must at the outset distinguish affirmative action entailing preferences from nondiscrimination, a principle that simply requires one to refrain from treating people differently because of their race, ethnicity, or other protected characteristics. Although this distinction can blur at the edges, it is clear and vital both in politics and in principle.

When affirmative action became federal policy in the late 1960s, the nondiscrimination principle, though fragile, was gaining strength. Preferences, by contrast, were flatly rejected by civil rights leaders like Hubert Humphrey, Ted Kennedy, and Martin Luther King, Jr. In the three decades that followed, more and more Americans came to embrace nondiscrimination and to oppose affirmative action, yet as John Skrentny shows in his *Ironies of Affirmative Action,* federal bureaucrats extended affirmative action with little public notice or debate. Today, nondiscrimination, or equal opportunity, is a principle questioned by only a few bigots and extreme libertarians, and civil rights law is far-reaching and remedially robust. In contrast, affirmative action is widely seen as a demand for favoritism or even equal outcomes.

SOCIAL GAINS BY BLACKS

Blacks, the intended beneficiaries of affirmative action, are no longer the insular minority they were in the 1960s. Harvard sociologist Orlando Patterson shows their "astonishing" progress on almost every front. "A mere 13% of the population," he notes, "Afro-Americans dominate the nation's popular culture. . . . [A]t least 35 percent of Afro-American adult, male workers are solidly middle class." The income of young, intact black families approaches that of demographically similar whites. On almost every other social index (residential integration is a laggard), the black-white gap is narrowing significantly; indeed, the income gap for young black women has disappeared.

Even these comparisons understate black progress. Much of racism's cruel legacy is permanently impounded in the low education and income levels of older blacks who grew up under Jim Crow; their economic disadvantages pull down the averages, obscuring the gains of their far better-educated children and grandchildren. These gains, moreover, have coincided with the arrival of record numbers of immigrants who are competing with blacks. To ignore this factor, economist Robert Lerner says, is like analyzing inequality trends in Germany since 1990 without noting that it had absorbed an entire impoverished country, East Germany. In addition, comparisons that fail to age-adjust social statistics obscure the fact that blacks, whose average age is much lower than that of whites, are less likely to have reached their peak earning years.

My point, emphatically, is not that blacks have achieved social equality—far from it—but that the situation facing them today is altogether different than it was when affirmative action was adopted. Advocates, of course, say that this progress just proves that affirmative action is effective; hence it should be continued or even increased. But this post hoc ergo propter hoc reasoning is fallacious and ignores the policy's growing incoherence and injustice.

SIZE, BENEFICIARIES,
AND CONSEQUENCES OF PREFERENCES

When we weigh competing claims for scarce resources—jobs, admission to higher education, public and private contracts, broadcast or other spectrum licenses, credit, housing, and the like—how heavy is the thumb that affirmative action places on the scales? This is a crucial question. The larger the preference, the more it conflicts with competing interests and values, especially the ideal of merit—almost regardless of how one defines merit.

The best data concern higher education admissions where (for better or for worse) schools commonly use standardized test scores as a proxy for aptitude, preparation, and achievement. William Bowen and Derek Bok, the former presidents of Princeton and Harvard, published a study in 1999 based largely on the academic records of more than 80,000 students who entered 28 highly selective institutions in three different years. Affirmative action, they claimed, only applies to these institutions, although a more recent study suggests that the practice now extends to some second- and even third-tier schools.

Selective institutions, of course, take other factors into account besides race. Indeed, some whites who are admitted have worse academic credentials than the blacks admitted under preferences. Still, Bowen and Bok find a difference of almost 200 points in the average SAT scores of the black and white applicants, and even this understates the group difference. First, the deficit for black applicants' high school grade point average (GPA), the other main admission criterion, is even larger. Thomas Kane finds that black applicants to selective schools "enjoy an advantage equivalent to an increase of two-thirds of a point in [GPA]—on a four-point scale—or [the equivalent of] 400 points on the SAT." Second, although the SAT is often criticized as culturally biased against blacks, SAT (and GPA) scores at every level actually overpredict their college performance. Third, the odds were approximately even that black applicants with scores between 1100 and 1199 would be admitted, whereas the odds for whites did not reach that level until they had scores in the 1450–1499 range. With a score of 1500 or above, more than a third of whites were rejected while every single black gained admission. The University of Michigan, whose affirmative action program is detailed in a pending lawsuit, weighs race even more heavily than the average school in the Bowen and Bok sample. At Michigan, being black, Hispanic, or Native American gives one the equivalent of a full point of GPA; minority status can override any SAT score deficit. And a recent study of 47 public institutions found that the odds of a black student being admitted compared to a white student with the same SAT and GPA were 173 to 1 at Michigan and 177 to 1 at North Carolina State.

These preferences, then, are not merely tie-breakers; they are huge—and they continue at the graduate and professional school levels. It is encouraging that an identical share (56 percent) of black and white graduates of the institutions in the Bowen and Bok sample earned graduate degrees; the share of blacks earning professional or doctoral degrees was actually slightly higher than for whites (40 percent vs. 37 percent). But black students' college grades and postgraduate test scores are so much lower on average that their admission to these programs, disproportionately at top-tier institutions, also depends on affirmative action. In the early 1990s, for example, only a few dozen of the 420 blacks admitted to the 18 most selective law schools would have been admitted absent affirmative action. A high percentage of these schools' black graduates eventually pass the bar examination, but some 22 percent of blacks' from these schools who take the exam never pass it (compared with 3 percent of whites), and only 61 percent of blacks pass it the first time compared with 92 percent of whites. Blacks who enter the professions do enjoy solid status, income, civic participation and leadership, and career satisfaction. But this hardly makes the case for affirmative action, for the higher-scoring applicants whom they displaced would presumably have done at least as well.

How much of blacks' impressive gains is due to reduced discrimination resulting from changing white attitudes and civil rights enforcement, as distinct from preferences? How would they have fared had they attended the somewhat less prestigious schools they could have attended without preferences? What would the demographics of higher education be without those preferences? We cannot answer these vital questions conclusively. We know that black gains were substantial even before preferences were adopted, that preference beneficiaries are overwhelmingly from middle- and upper-class families, and that most black leaders in all walks of life did not go to elite universities. We also know that many institutions are so committed to affirmative action that they will find ways to prefer favored groups—minorities, legacies, athletes, and others-no matter what the formal rules say. Although California voters banned affirmative action in state programs, their politicians press the university system to jigger the admission criteria until it finds a formula that can skirt the ban and produce the "correct" number of the favored minorities (excluding Asians, who are thought not to need the help).

NEW DEMOGRAPHIC REALITIES

The moral case for affirmative action rests on the bitter legacy of black slavery, Jim Crow, and the violent dispossession of Native Americans. Yet the descendants of slaves and Native Americans constitute a shrinking share of affirmative action's beneficiaries. Political logrolling has extended preferential treatment to the largest immigrant group, Hispanics, as well as to blacks from Africa, the Caribbean, and elsewhere, Asians and Pacific Islanders, and in some programs to women, a majority group.

Some affirmative action advocates acknowledge this problem and want to fix it.

Orlando Patterson, for example, would exclude "first-generation persons of African ancestry" but not "their children and later generations . . . in light of the persistence of racist discrimination in America." He would also exclude all Hispanics except for Puerto Ricans and Mexican Americans of second or later generations and would exclude "all Asians except Chinese-Americans descended from pre-1923 immigrants. . . ." With due respect for Patterson's path-breaking work on race, his formula resembles a tax code provision governing depreciation expenses more than a workable formula for promoting social justice.

Centuries of immigration and intermarriage have rendered the conventional racial categories ever more meaningless. The number of Americans who consider themselves multiracial and who wish to be identified as such (if they must be racially identified at all) was 7 million in the 2000 census, including nearly 2 million blacks (5 percent of the black population) and 37 percent of all Native Americans. This is why advocacy groups who are desperate to retain the demographic status quo lobbied furiously to preempt a multiracial category.

In perhaps the most grimly ironic aspect of the new demographic dispensation, the government adopted something like the one-drop rule that helped enslave mulattos and self-identifying whites before Emancipation. Under OMB'S rules, any response combining one minority race and the white race must be allocated to the minority race. This, although 25 percent of those in the United States who describe themselves as both black and white consider themselves white, as do almost half of Asian-white people and more than 80 percent of Indian-white people. The lesson is clear: making our social policy pivot on the standard racial categories is both illogical and politically unsustainable.

ALTERNATIVES

Even a remote possibility that eliminating affirmative action would resegregate our society deeply distresses almost all Americans. Nothing else can explain the persistence of a policy that, contrary to basic American values, distributes valuable social resources according to skin color and surname. But to say that we must choose between perpetuating affirmative action and eliminating it entirely is false. To be sure, most suggested reforms—using social class or economic disadvantage rather than race, choosing among minimally qualified students by lottery, and making preferences temporary—are impracticable or would make matters worse. Limiting affirmative action to the descendants of slaves and Native Americans would minimize some objections to the policy but, as Patterson's proposal suggests, would be tricky to implement and would still violate the nondiscrimination and merit principles.

Most Americans who favor affirmative action would probably concede that it fails to treat the underlying problem. Black applicants will continue to have worse academic credentials until they can attend better primary and secondary schools and receive the remediation they need. A root cause of their disadvantage is inferior schooling, and affirmative action is simply a poultice. We must often deal with symptoms rather than root causes because we do not know how to eliminate them, or consider it too costly to do so, or cannot muster the necessary political will. If we know which social or educational reforms can substantially improve low-income children's academic performance, then we should by all mean adopt them. But this does not mean that we should preserve affirmative action until we can eliminate the root causes of inequality.

I propose instead that we treat governmental, legally mandated preferences differently than private, voluntary ones. While prohibiting the former (except in the narrow remedial context approved by the Supreme Court), I would permit the latter—but only under certain conditions discussed below. A liberal society committed to freedom and private autonomy has good reasons to maintain this difference; racial preferences imposed by law are pernicious in ways that private ones are not. To affirmative action advocates, it is a Catch-22 to bar the benign use of race now after having used it against minorities for centuries. But to most Americans (including many minorities), affirmative action is not benign. It is not Catch-22 to recognize what history teaches—that race is perhaps the worst imaginable category around which to organize political and social relations. The social changes I have described only reinforce this lesson. A public law that affirms our common values should renounce the distributive use of race, not perpetuate it.

There are other differences between public and private affirmative action. A private preference speaks for and binds only those who adopt it and only for as long as they retain it. It does not serve, as public law should, as a social ideal. As I explained in *The Limits of Law: Essays on Democratic Governance* (2000), legal rules tend to be cruder, more simplistic, slower to develop, and less contextualized than voluntary ones, which are tailored to more specific needs and situations. Legal rules reflect interest group politics or the vagaries of judicial decision; voluntary ones reflect the chooser's own assessment of private benefits and costs. Legal rules are more difficult to reform, abandon, or escape. Voluntary ones can assume more diverse forms than mandated ones, a diversity that facilitates social learning and problem solving.

Still, many who believe in nondiscrimination and merit and who conscientiously weigh the competing values still support affirmative action. If a private university chooses to sacrifice some level of academic performance to gain greater racial diversity and whatever educational or other values it thinks diversity will bring, I cannot say—nor should the law say—that its choice is impermissible. Because even private affirmative action violates the nondiscrimination principle, however, I would permit it only on two conditions: transparency and protection of minorities. First, the preference—its criteria, weights, and reasons—must be fully disclosed. If it cannot withstand public criticism, it should be scrapped. The goal is to discipline preferences by forcing institutions to reveal their value choices. This will trigger market, reputational, and other informal mechanisms that make them bear more of the policy's costs rather than just shifting them surreptitiously to nonpreferred applicants, as they do now. Second, private affirmative action must not disadvantage a group to which the Constitution affords heightened protection. A preference favoring whites, for example, would violate this condition.

THE COMMITMENT TO LEGAL EQUALITY

For better and for worse, American culture remains highly individualistic in its values and premises, even at some sacrifice (where sacrifice is necessary) to its goal of substantive equality. The illiberal strands in our tangled history that enslaved, excluded, and subordinated individuals as members of racial groups should chasten our efforts to use race as a distributive criterion. Affirmative action in its current form, however well-intended, violates the distinctive, deeply engrained cultural and moral commitments to legal equality, private autonomy, and enhanced opportunity that have served Americans well—even though they have not yet served all of us equally well.

Peter H. Schuck is professor of law at Yale University and New York University. This article is drawn from a chapter in a forthcoming book, Diversity in America: Keeping Government at a Safe Distance *(Harvard).*

CRITICAL THINKING QUESTIONS

1. How has the Supreme Court shaped affirmative action?
2. What is the first "structural change" the author would make in affirmative action? How does he justify it?
3. What is the second "structural change" the author would make in affirmative action? And how does he justify this?
4. What are your own opinions on affirmative action? How do you justify them?

6

Public Opinion and Political Socialization

How to Spot a Bogus Poll

Brad Edmondson

Opinion surveys can look convincing and be completely worthless. But asking four simple questions of any poll can separate the good numbers from the trash.

Politicians use opinion polls as verbal weapons in campaign ads. Journalists use them as props to liven up infotainment shows. Executives are more likely to pay attention to polls when the numbers support their decisions. But this isn't how polls are meant to be used. Opinion polls can be a good way to learn about the views Americans hold on important subjects, but only if you know how to cut through the contradictions and confusion.

Conducting surveys is difficult. It is especially difficult to take a meaningful survey of public opinion, because opinion is a subjective thing that can change rapidly from day to day. Poll questions sometimes produce conflicting or meaningless results, even when they are carefully written and presented by professional interviewers to scientifically chosen samples.

That's why the best pollsters sweat the details on the order and wording of questions, and the way data are coded, analyzed, and tabulated.

Pollsters other than the best can also set up surveys that deliberately shade the truth. They do this by acting like trial lawyers: they ask leading questions, or they restrict their questions to people likely to give the desired response. In fact, pollsters can use dozens of obscure tricks to intentionally push the results

American Demographics, Oct 1996, v18, n10, p10(5).

© 1996 Intertec Publishing Corporation, A PRIMEDIA Co.

of a survey in the desired direction. So the next time a poker-faced person tries to give you the latest news about how Americans feel, ask some pointed questions of your own.

Did You Ask the Right People? In 1936, the editors of *Literary Digest* conducted a Presidential preference poll of more than 2 million Americans. The poll predicted that the Republican candidate, Alf Landon, would defeat Franklin Roosevelt. Landon's loss made the *Digest* history's most famous victim of sample bias.

The *Digest* mailed more than 10 million ballots to households listed in telephone books and automobile registration records. This method might create a relatively representative sample today, but in 1936, it substantially biased the sample toward those affluent enough to own cars and phones. The magazine's disgrace was made complete by young poll-takers like George Gallup and Elmo Roper, who used samples of a few thousand people to predict a Roosevelt win.

Gallup and Roper carefully chose their samples to reflect a demographic cross-section of Americans, just as they do today.

The most amazing thing about this story is that some journalists and businesses in the 1990s still make the mistakes the *Literary Digest* made 60 years ago. Any journalist with half a pencil knows now that only a scientifically chosen survey sample will represent the country's opinions. But the temptation to take a biased poll is great if you have a tight deadline and a small budget, as many news organizations do.

The 2 million who responded to the *Literary Digest* poll in 1936 were even more likely than the total sample base to be wealthy and Republican, typifying a common survey problem—nonresponse bias. Even when you start out with a representative sample, you could end up with a biased one. This is a risk all pollsters take, but some particular methods lend themselves to greater error. For example, readers of women's magazines are frequently asked to fill out surveys on weighty subjects like crime and sexual behavior. Not only do such polls ignore the opinions of nonreaders, they are biased toward readers who take the trouble to fill out and return the questionnaire, usually at their own expense.

Television news and entertainment shows get into the act by posting toll-free or even toll numbers that viewers can call to "vote" on an issue. These samples are not only biased, they are prone to "ballot-stuffing" by enthusiasts. In other words, viewers who call 12 times get 12 votes.

Poll results based on "convenience" samples can be wildly misleading, even if the sample sizes are huge. A call-in poll conducted by a television network in 1983 asked: "Should the United Nations continue to be based in the United States?" About 185,000 calls were received. Two-thirds said that the U.N. should move. At the same time, the network conducted a random-sample poll of 1,000 people, and only 28 percent said the U.N. should move.

Between 1989 and 1995, the Pew Research Center for The People & The Press in Washington, D.C., monitored the public's interest in 480 major news stories. Almost half of Americans paid little or no attention to these stories, and only one in four followed the average story very closely. Stories about wars and disasters were followed most closely, while those about celebrity scandals and politics finished last. When Pat Buchannan announced that he was running for President in 1991, for example, only 7 percent of Americans paid close attention to the story.

Conflicts Make News. When journalists are trying to liven up a boring political story, they need angry, well-informed citizens like a fish needs water. This is one reason why older men may be quoted more often than other groups. Those aged 50 and older are more likely than younger adults to follow news stories "very closely," according to the Center, and men are more likely than women to follow stories about war, business, sports, and politics.

In the last decade, angry white men have dominated media programs designed to give ordinary people a chance to speak out in public. Two-thirds of regular listeners to political talk radio programs are men, according to a 1996 poll taken by Roper Starch Worldwide for the Media Studies Center in New York City. Republicans outnumber Democrats three to one in the talk-radio audience, and 89 percent of listeners are white, compared with the national average for voters of 83 percent. Three in five regular listeners to political talk radio perceive a liberal bias in the mainstream media, compared with one in five nonlisteners.

A multitude of reputable surveys have shown that most Americans generally believe that the country is headed in the wrong direction and that political leaders can't be trusted. But those who respond to convenience polls and call in to talk shows probably don't speak for most Americans.

What's the margin? A statistician and two friends are hunting for deer. They spot a buck. Friend number one takes a shot and hits a tree five feet to the left of the animal. Friend number two fires and hits a tree five feet to the right. The statistician exclaims, "We got him!"

No matter how carefully a survey sample is chosen, there will still be some margin of error. If you selected ten different sets of 1,000 people using the same rules and asked each group the same question, the results would not be identical. The difference between the results is sampling error. Statisticians know that the error is equally likely to be above or below the true mark, and that larger samples have smaller margins of error if they are properly drawn. They are also able to estimate the margin of error, or the amount by which the result could be above or below the truth. Sampling error will always exist unless you survey every member of a population. If you do that, you have conducted a census.

Sampling error is one reason why two professionally conducted polls can show different results and both be correct. For example, the CNN/*USA Today*/Gallup Poll of January 5–7, 1996, showed that the proportion of Americans who approved of President Clinton's performance had dropped to 42 percent, from 51 percent on December 15–18, 1995. Polls conducted that same week by *Washington Post*/ABC and *New York Times*/CBS showed that his approval rating was 53 percent and 50 percent, respectively. This made for a few wild days at the White House, until the next Gallup survey showed a sudden rebound.

Reputable surveys report a margin of error—usually of 3 or 4 percentage points—at a particular confidence level—typically 95 percent. This means that 5 percent of the time, or 1 time in 20, the poll's results will not be reliable. The other 95 percent of the time, it is within 3 or 4 percentage points of the "truth." This sort of inevitable statistical problem explains the blip in the January Gallup poll.

Which Came First? The order in which questions are asked can have a big effect on the results. In late May 1996, the CNN/*USA Today*/Gallup poll reported that 55 percent of Americans believe taxes can be cut and the federal deficit reduced at the same time, compared with 39 percent who do not believe this. The same week, New York Times/CBS reported a dead heat of 46 percent who believe and 46 percent who do not. This variance was way beyond the margin of error. The questions were almost identical in their wording. But the order of questions in the Gallup poll may have biased the results, according to Poll Watch, a publication of the Pew Research Center.

In the CBS poll, questions before the tax cut/deficit question were not related to the subject. But Gallup first asked respondents if they favor a tax cut. Then it asked those who did if they would still favor it even if it meant no reduction in the deficit. Then it asked all respondents if they believed both could be done at the same time. By that point, "some of Gallup's interviewees may have felt invested in the idea of a tax cut," says Poll Watch.

Most people want to appear consistent to others and to be consistent in their own minds. When a pollster asks a series of related questions, this desire can lead people to take positions they might not have taken if they were asked only one question. Neither way produces an obviously "correct" response, but the results are different. One way to handle this problem is to rotate the order of questions. Then the degree of differences due to question order can be described and interpreted. But not everyone pays heed to such fine distinctions.

What Was the Question? "Do you want union officials, in effect, to decide how many municipal employees you, the taxpayer, must support?" Well, do you? This question, taken from an actual survey, is obviously biased. The results might make good propaganda for an anti-union group, but they are totally bogus as a poll. So before you pass a survey finding on to others, or even believe it yourself, be sure to look at the actual question.

Question wording is extremely subtle. In the hours after President Clinton's November 27, 1995, speech announcing that 20,000 U.S. troops would be sent to Bosnia as part of a NATO peace-keeping mission, three major news organizations took reaction polls. CNN/*USA Today*/Gallup found that 46 percent of Americans favored Clinton's plan, while 40 percent were opposed. CBS found that only 33 percent were in favor, and 58 percent were opposed. ABC said that 39 percent were in favor, and 57 percent were opposed.

The CNN poll was probably more in favor because it did not mention that the U.S. was sending 20,000 troops, says Poll Watch. CBS and ABC gave respondents the chance to react to that substantial number, which drove down their approval. In addition, CBS described the troops' mission as "enforcing the peace agreement," while ABC and CNN described the troops as part of "an international peace-keeping force." CBS's harsher wording may have contributed to its respondents' harsher judgment of the Clinton decision.

Sometimes words are problematic because they are too vague. In April 1996, the Pew Research Center asked which Presidential candidate was best described by the phrase: "shares my values." By this measure, Clinton beat Dole by 47 percent to 37 percent. But when CBS and the *New York Times* asked whether each candidate "shares the moral values most Americans try to live by," 70 percent said that Dole did, but only 59 percent said so of Clinton.

One way to sharpen the meaning of a poll on "values" is to ask an open-ended question, such as: "What 'values' do you share with the candidate?" The long list of responses generated by such a question can be entered and coded to provide the sample's average definition of the term. This step obviously takes more time and money. It produces a survey that is more precise, but harder to explain. If you were a television reporter and you had 20 seconds to describe the question and give the result, what would you do?

These are some of the most common reasons why polls that appear to be authoritative are, in fact, total trash. Other pitfalls are described in *Polls and Surveys: Understanding What They Tell Us*, a layperson's guide by Norman M. Bradburn and Seymour Sudman (San Francisco: Jossey-Bass, Inc., 1988). The Pew Research Center's Poll Watch newsletter does an excellent job of spotting and explaining poll gaffes: for more information, call Pew at (202) 293-3126.

When you're presented with a new survey or a used car, it helps to ask a few key questions before you buy. But for all their flaws, surveys are essential to the work of politicians, journalists, and businesspeople. "Yes, there are too many bad polls" writes Richard Morin, director of polling for the Washington Post. There are also "too many polls that report what people think but not why they think it."

At the same time, with lots of competing polls, it's easier to see errors and rapid shifts in public opinion. "Polling is a robust methodology," writes Morin. "A lot of little things can go wrong and the final result can still be right, or at least close enough."

CRITICAL THINKING QUESTIONS

1. What are common examples of "bogus" polls?
2. What is sampling error and how can it affect poll accuracy?
3. How can the ordering of poll questions affect poll accuracy?
4. How can the wording of poll questions affect poll accuracy?

7

Interest Groups

MoveOn's Big Moment

Chris Taylor and Karen Tumulty

F ew Democratic campaigns can boast matching funds from megarich
financier George Soros, feisty speeches by Al Gore and a make-your-
own-campaign-commercial contest conceived by pop star Moby. These
are the trophies of MoveOn.org, an activist website with just seven staff members and no office. What it does have is an e-mail list with 1.8 million members, who have little more in common than anger and a tilt to the left.

The seven staff members focus that anger on the liberal topic du jour. One
day, MoveOn's e-mail armada pushes a petition against the FCC's relaxing
rules on media ownership; the next, a fund drive that brought in $1 million in
48 hours to support the Texas state senators who had fled the state to stop a
G.O.P. redistricting plan. There are no membership dues, and gratification is
as instant as a mouse click. "MoveOn is easily the largest political-action
committee in the country," says Professor Michael Cornfield of George
Washington University. "It's the Christian Coalition of the left."

MoveOn's latest campaign is its most ambitious—a $10 million drive to fund
anti–Bush commercials in key battleground states later this month. Billionaires
Soros and Peter Lewis last week offered to give $1 for every $2 given by members, up to a cap of $5 million. Meanwhile, Moby and a host of celebrity pals (like
Jack Black and Janeane Garafolo) are getting ready to judge the best commercial
made by members, which MoveOn will air around the State of the Union.

All this began with Wes Boyd and Joan Blades, a married couple of
Berkeley-based computer entrepreneurs whose company was best known for

Time, Nov 24, 2003, v162, i21, p32.

"MoveOn's Big Movement…" by Chris Taylor and Karen Tumulty. © 2003 Time Inc.,
reprinted by permission.

a screensaver that featured flying toasters. In 1997 they sold it for $13.8 million. Then came impeachment. Wes and Joan put together a website and sent it to friends. Its title and policy: Censure and Move On. As an afterthought, the couple put together an e-mail list of supporters. "It was supposed to be a flash campaign," says Wes. "We're in, we're out, we're fixed."

But they were hooked. By 2000, MoveOn.org was raising $2 million for Democratic candidates, including more than $100,000 to help California's Adam Schiff beat Congressman James Rogan, one of the House managers during Clinton's impeachment trial. In mid-to late 2002, as the Iraq war loomed, the MoveOn e-mail list doubled, to 1 million. Wes and Joan hooked up with Zack Exley, whose parody campaign 2000 website, GWBush.com, caused candidate Bush to declare, "There ought to be some limits to freedom"; and Eli Pariser, 22, a New Yorker whose post-9/11 e-mail petition for peace was signed by 500,000 people worldwide. All four still work out of their homes, communicating by e-mail, instant messaging and a regular Tuesday conference call.

In June, MoveOn held what was billed as the first Internet presidential primary, and more than 317,000 members voted. Former Vermont Governor Howard Dean grabbed the top spot with 44%—not quite the 50% MoveOn required to endorse a candidate but enough to give his candidacy the momentum it still enjoys. Dean's rivals grumbled that MoveOn had advised Dean on how to market himself to its members. Exley says the site had made the same offer to others, but "back then, the Dean campaign was the only one desperate enough to take us up on it."

Now Wes and Joan's quiet Berkeley home plays host to a steady stream of consultants and candidates coming to pay homage. Those who seek endorsement are in for a disappointment. "I don't spend any time figuring out who the right candidate is," says Wes. "All I want to do is evangelize populism, so they go away thinking 'Whoa—there's someone other than wealthy donors I have to impress?'"

CRITICAL THINKING QUESTIONS

1. How is MoveOn.org described in this article?
2. What techniques does MoveOn.org use to raise campaign funds?

8

Political Parties

Third Parties and the Two-Party System

Christian Collet

Since the late 1960s and early 1970s, there has been much discussion and concern about the stability and strength of the two-party system in America. After David Broder's (1971) declaration that "the party's over," a debate emerged among political scientists and observers over whether the Republicans and Democrats—and partisanship itself—were indeed in decline. In large part, the focus on party decline has generated ample evidence of increasing voter independence since 1952 (e.g., Beck 1984; Nie, Verba, and Petrocik 1979; Wattenberg 1996), although some controversy remains about whether voters may actually be "covert partisans" (Keith et al. 1992, p. 23). For those looking at general public support for the party system, though, there has been less controversy. As Jack Dennis concluded in a 1975 article that looked at most of the available indicators of party system strength over time, "attitudes toward the parties and the evaluations of the importance of the party institution show, with few exceptions, a general state of low public regard and legitimation" (p. 218). While some have argued that the Republicans and Democrats have revitalized organizationally and have become increasingly competitive (e.g., Herrnson 1994; Reichley 1994), few would conclude that, generally speaking, the major parties and the two-party system are as sacred to the American public today as they once were.

Recently, the discussion of party system instability has taken on a new twist with the emergence of Ross Perot and the increasing activity of third parties

Public Opinion Quarterly, Fall 1996, v60, n3, p431(19).

© 1996 University of Chicago Press.

and independent candidates. While the candidacies of George Wallace and John Anderson in the 1968 and 1980 presidential elections attracted some attention to the existent strains in the system, it was not until Perot's surprising 19 percent showing in 1992 that the cracks in the two-party armor began to be fully apparent and alternatives to the Republicans and Democrats credibly considered. Following Perot, a number of political observers—Theodore Lowi (1994) and Gordon Black and Benjamin Black (1994) among them—began to argue for the creation of a third major party, citing strong public support that they claim exists for a viable, mainstream alternative. In September 1995, Ross Perot began to transform the possibility into reality, by announcing the formation of his Reform Party and launching a campaign to qualify it for the ballot in all fifty states. In the course of his announcement and efforts to get his party registered nationwide, he, like Lowi and Black and Black, cited public opinion data showing overwhelming support for a third party. "Sixty-two percent of the American voters," Perot claimed in ads and speeches, "want a new political party."

The available trend data on the two-party system reveal that, on some indicators, the "general state of low public regard" for the parties found by Dennis in 1975 has sunk even lower. In an NES item asking whether parties "make the government pay attention to what the people think," the percentage saying "not much" has grown from a mere 13 percent in 1964 to 30 percent in 1995, when the question was repeated by CBS/*New York Times* (question 1 below). Another important NES measure of party attitudes—the feeling thermometer—also evidences growing disenchantment; those feeling cold toward the Democrats and, more important, political parties in general, have shot to unprecedented levels since 1990 (question 2; feelings toward the Republicans, however, have been stable). On the positive side for the parties, there has been no substantial increase over time in the percentage of those agreeing with the idea that "we probably don't need political parties" (question 3). Further, the likes and dislikes measured by NES show no net increase in negative feelings toward the specific parties since 1952 (question 4), although they do underscore the trend toward neutrality, as Wattenberg (1996) has observed.

Those seeing "no difference" between the parties were no higher in 1994 than in 1952 (question 5), and there was no change from 1978 to 1984 in the nearly two-thirds agreeing that there are at least "some basic differences" between the two parties (question 6). However, from 1981 to 1985 nearly two-thirds consistently agreed that the "two political parties do more to confuse the issues than to provide a clear choice" (question 7). Thus, while the public may recognize fundamental distinctions between the parties, they seem to be increasingly indifferent toward them when asked to evaluate them individually. When respondents are asked to evaluate the two-party "system" or the "two political parties" as a whole, though, the public mood tends to move from neutrality to negativity.

Recent items asking respondents to make more direct assessments about the party system underscore this point. A question asked twice by the *Los Angeles Times* in 1995 (question 8), shows that roughly half of the public consider the two-party system to be "unsound." Some other questions that have not been repeated suggest similar dissatisfaction; one, in particular, by NBC/*Wall Street Journal* in 1995 showed that only 15 percent agreed that the "two-party system works fairly well," and 82 percent said it has either "real problems" or "is seriously broken" (9/16-19/95). Another by Gordon Black in 1992 showed 56 percent agreeing that they "were angry at both political parties" (5/92). Thus, the public may not feel greater dissaffection toward the Republicans and Democrats in particular—61 percent in 1992 CBS/*New York Times* poll said that "the Republican and Democratic parties are still necessary" (6/17-20/92)—but are registering a growing antipathy toward the two-party system and its ability to provide compelling ideas and solutions to the chronic problems in the nation.

We can observe some of this growing desire for alternatives by observing the increasing levels of public support for a third party. However, the available trend data in this area are somewhat problematic, for two reasons: (1) many items are inconsistent in terms of question wording and frequency, and it has only been in recent years that identical questions on third parties have been asked with regularity; (2) in large part, items seem to be asked in periods where third party movements are making noise, which may mean that public hostility toward the two-party system and support for third parties may be artificially high (since they are measured only at high points). This makes it difficult to develop firm generalizations about the strength and consistency of support for third parties over time.

Still, the data do reveal some considerable changes. The earliest items on third parties (appearing in Roper surveys in 1938 and 1944) show overwhelming majorities in support for and satisfaction with the two-party system (questions 9–10), and the support for the current system continued to be strong into the 1960s—even as Wallace emerged and voters began to act more independently, in terms of self-identification and ticket splitting (Nie, Verba, and Petrocik 1979). But by the early eighties, the drop in support for the system began to manifest, and by 1994, for the first time, a minority said that they felt that the Republicans and Democrats were doing "an adequate job" and a majority felt that there should "be a third major party."

Additional questions highlight the change that occurred between the 1960s and today. Similarly worded Gallup and Harris items show increases between the 1960s and the 1980s in the number who would support a "center" or "middle-of-the-road" party (question 11). More illustrative of the current situation is a question asked by ABC/*Washington Post* in the 1980s and repeated, with a small variation, by Times-Mirror in 1994 and 1995, asking whether respondents agree or disagree with the statement "We should have a third major political party in this country in addition to the Republicans and Democrats."

In the early 1980s, support ranged from 41 to 49 percent, and the percentages declined as low as 37 percent in 1985 (question 12). But when Times–Mirror asked a similar, though not identical, question in a 1994 survey, they found that 53 percent agreed; by October 1995, the percentage had grown to 59 percent. Yet another item asked in 1992 and continued at several points throughout 1995 and early 1996 by CBS/*New York Times* showed roughly the same levels of support for third parties, with fairly stable agreement in the mid to upper fifties (question 13).

Other items have shown even greater percentages supporting the idea of a third party. *Time*/CNN surveys by Yankelovich have asked a differently worded question that has tended to get higher rates of approval: "Would you favor or oppose the formation of a third political party that would run candidates for president, Congress, and state office against the Republican and Democratic candidates?" (question 14). Those in favor grew from 58 percent in June 1992 to as high as 63 percent in October 1992 but fell off to 50–59 percent in the 1993 to early 1995 period. A similarly worded item asked in late 1995 by ABC/*Washington Post* (question 15), though, shows overall support rebounding to over 60 percent but only 25 to 31 percent saying that they were "strongly" in support of a third party. In general, it seems that the higher percentages of support elicited by these two questions may underscore the public's interest, in particular, in having more candidates to choose from during election time; rather than having a single alternative in the presidential election, they may be asking for more alternatives across the board. Affirming this point is a follow-up to a CBS/*New York Times* survey (12/95) that asked why individuals said they wanted "a new political party." Seventy-five percent said that it was because "having more [candidates] is better for the country," while only 16 percent said that it was because the two parties did not "produce good candidates."(1) As well, a more recent CBS/*New York Times* survey in April 1996 showed a plurality (48 percent) agreeing that "having only two parties can't provide voters with enough options."(2)

While Perot and others can take satisfaction that the public has become more receptive to the general idea of having a third party, especially one that they feel will offer more candidates and choice on the ballot, some questions remain about the depth, stability, and viability of support for such an alternative. Can support for the idea of a third party, in general, translate into support for a specific party at the polls? Traditionally, third party candidates for the presidency fare well early in campaigns but usually see their support diminish considerably before Election Day (question 16), as voters begin to sense that they do not have a realistic chance at winning the race (Abramson et al. 1995; Rosenstone, Behr, and Lazarus 1984). (Colin Powell, who was getting consistent levels of support before he bowed out of the campaign last November, may have been an exception, however [question 17].) Furthermore, none of the significant third party or independent candidates in recent years has been able to establish an enduring top-to-bottom party organization capable of mounting a consistent slate of candidates in statewide and legislative elections.(3)

There also seems to be some doubt about whether the public thinks that an alternative party or parties are the best way to remedy the "system" or whether there may be greater support for political independence. When asked to choose between maintaining the two-party system, having elections without party labels, or having "one or more new parties" emerge, support for the latter drops, with a low of 23 percent in the most recent asking of this question in the 1994 NES (question 18). By contrast, support for elections without party labels has been consistently around one-third, while the percentage wanting to maintain the two-party system increased significantly, from 29 percent to 39 percent between 1992 and 1994. In another item, the public has consistently shown a two to one preference for "independent" candidates over "party" candidates, when the question was asked between 1974 and 1986 (question 19). Feeling thermometer ratings indicate (question 20) that "independents" have generally had greater positive than negative ratings, although this may have changed slightly in recent years as an increasingly unpopular Perot has become more closely identified with independents. More recently, the public showed a strong desire for Colin Powell to mount a presidential campaign independent of any party affiliation (question 21).

Since few are willing to give unqualified support to any third party candidate (question 22), a major problem for Perot and others is convincing the public that a third party can make a difference in terms of governing. Recent items by CNN/*USA Today* and CBS/*New York Times* show, respectively, that the public is skeptical about a new party's ability to solve the problems that afflict Washington; 48 percent feel that Perot's party would "continue politics as usual" and 49 percent believe that a third party would lead to "more conflict."(4) Furthermore, most feel it to be "very" or "somewhat" important that the president "be from one of the two major parties," and this has changed little between 1980 and 1995 (question 23). Sixty-one percent feel that a president who was neither a Republican nor Democrat would have "serious problems" dealing with Congress.(5)

In sum, the data provided here do show increases in discontent with the two-party system and an increase in the willingness to support a third party, as Perot, Black and Black, and others have claimed. But some tendencies in the data ought to be considered. First, it is important to remember that the public shows more antipathy toward the "system" itself—the two parties together in an abstract sense—rather than the Republicans and Democrats in particular. Their support for a third party seems to be rooted in a desire for more choices at the polls rather than any deep-seated desire to replace, or do away with, the existing choices. Second, support for a third party diminishes when respondents are given a choice between nonpartisan reforms and a party movement (question 18). Third, while the public shows an interest in third parties in an electoral sense, they have some serious reservations about their abilities to govern; even in 1992, when third party support was running high, most continued to believe that it is important that the president "be from one of the two major parties" (question 23).

Ultimately, it is difficult to know whether the country is merely in the midst of a period of extreme discontent that will eventually subside or whether public angst will persist until genuine structural change occurs. The data suggest that the desire for change is there—and the gradual and dramatic increase in public support for the idea of another party is certainly strong evidence—but questions remain as to whether that support for the idea of having a third party can be maintained for a particular party itself. Support for alternative parties and candidates at the national level has traditionally been fleeting, and any third party or independent candidate will face considerable challenges in convincing the public that he or she can govern a country dominated by the major parties and can make a lasting difference. The public may be more open these days to the general idea of having parties or independent candidates competing for office with Republicans and Democrats (which would presumably encourage more parties and candidates to do so), but there is no indication, at this point, that equal levels of support will exist for those parties or candidates if they do emerge, or if the support will sustain itself to have a lasting effect on American politics.

The survey data reported here were gathered from several published and unpublished sources, including Gallup Poll Monthly, the Roper Center for Public Opinion Research's POLL database, and the Inter-University Consortium for Political and Social Research (ICPSR). Additional information about these data can be obtained from the Roper Center, ICPSR, and the specific organizations listed in the appendix below.

APPENDIX

Sources and Abbreviations

ABC/WP: American Broadcasting Company/*Washington Post*

CBS/NYT: Columbia Broadcasting System/*New York Times*

CNN/USA: Cable News Network/*USA Today* surveys by Gallup

Harris: Louis Harris and Associates

Gallup: Gallup Organization

Greenberg: Greenberg Research/Democratic Leadership Council

LAT: Los Angeles Times

NBC/WSJ: National Broadcasting Corporation/*Wall Street Journal* by Hart and Teeter

NES: American National Election Studies, Center for Political Studies/Survey Research Center, ICPSR, University of Michigan

Newsweek: Newsweek surveys by Princeton Survey Research Associates

Roper: Roper Organization

Time/CNN: *Time Magazine*/Cable News Network surveys by Yankelovich

T-M: Times-Mirror Center for the People and the Press surveys by Princeton Survey Research Associates

USORC: U.S. Opinion Research Corporation

WP: *Washington Post*

1. CBS/*New York Times* (12/95) (asked only of those who said "Yes": "Do you say that (the country needs a new political party) mostly because you think neither the Republican nor the Democratic parties produce good candidates, or mostly because you think having more than two candidates to choose from is better for the country?" 16 percent: neither produces good candidates; 75 percent: having more is better for the country; 4 percent: other; 5 percent: don't know; N = 57 percent of original sample of 1,111.

2. CBS/*New York Times* (3/31–4/2/96): "Do you think having two parties gives voters enough options, or do you think that having only two parties can't provide voters with enough options?" 45 percent: gives enough options; 48 percent: too limited; 7 percent: don't know (DK) or no answer (N.A.); N = 1,257.

3. Perot's Reform Party has fielded some state and congressional candidates for the 1996 elections. Also, it should be noted that George Wallace's original American Independent Party (AIP) has persisted in California and continues to run a few candidates at the statewide and legislative level. Today, the party is under the umbrella of the U.S. Taxpayers' Party, a confederation of right-wing parties (some of which were formerly part of Wallace's original AIP before it fractured in the 1970s).

4. CNN/*USA Today* (9/26–27/95): "In your view, would the formation of a new national third party by Ross Perot create fundamental changes in the American political system, or would it just continue politics as usual?" 43 percent: create fundamental changes; 48 percent: continue politics as usual; 9 percent: DK or refused; N = 640. CBS/*New York Times* (8/5–9/95): "Do you think that if there were a third major political party there would be more conflict, less conflict, or wouldn't it make a difference one way or another?" 49 percent: more conflict; 12 percent: less conflict; 33 percent: no difference; 6 percent: DK or N.A.; N = 1,478.

5. CBS/*New York Times* (8/5-9/95): "Do you think a president who was not a Republican or Democrat could govern effectively, or do you think such a president would have serious problems dealing with Congress?" 61 percent: serious problems; 30 percent: govern effectively; 9 percent: DK; N = 1,478.

Christian Collet is a graduate student at University of California, Irvine. He thanks the Survey Research Center at University of California, Berkeley, and the Roper Center for their assistance in data compilation. He also thanks Mark Baldassare and, especially, Robert Shapiro for their advice and helpful comments on earlier drafts.

SURVEY RESULTS

Parties Help Government Pay Attention

1. NES, CBS/NYT: How much do you feel that political parties help to make the government pay attention to what the people think: a good deal, some, or not much?
[TABULAR DATA OMITTED]

Feeling Thermometers: Republican Party, Democratic Party, Political Parties in General

2. NES: I'd like to get your feelings toward some of our political leaders and other people who have been in the news. I'll read the name of a person and I'd like you to rate that person using something called the feeling thermometer.

You can choose any number between 0 and 100. The higher the number, the warmer or more favorable you feel toward that person; the lower the number, the colder or less favorable. You would rate the person at the 50 degree mark if you feel neither warm nor cold toward them. If we come to a person whose name you don't recognize, you don't need to rate that person. Just tell me and we'll move on to the next one. . . . How would you rate the following? . . . The Republican Party . . . the Democratic Party . . . political parties in general?
[TABULAR DATA OMITTED]

Need for Political Parties in America

3. NES: Next I will read some general statements about political parties.

Please use the scale on this page to tell me how strongly you agree or disagree with each statement. The scale runs from "disagree very strongly" at point 0 to "agree very strongly" at point 7. After I read each statement you can just give me the number from the scale that applies: The truth is we probably don't need political parties in America anymore (responses recorded).

	1980 (%)	1993 Pilot[a] (%)
Agree	30	33
Neutral	10	. . .
Disagree	52	66
DK	8	2
N	1,596	632

[a]Please tell me whether you agree or disagree with each of the following statements: The truth is we probably don't need political parties in America anymore. Do you agree strongly, agree somewhat, disagree somewhat, or disagree strongly?

Affection Toward Major Parties

4. NES: Is there anything that you (like/dislike) about the (Republican/Democratic) Party? [If yes] Anything else? [Based on the ratio of the total number of Republican and Democratic "likes" minus "dislikes" mentioned. NES coded as many as five likes and dislikes for each respondent. Ratio is negative (−) if total dislikes are greater than total likes and positive (+) if total number of likes mentioned are greater than number of dislikes. Ratio is neutral (0) if an equal number of likes and dislikes were mentioned. Columns contain the percentages falling into each of the three categories.]

	Republican Party			Democratic Party			
	−	0	+	−	0	+	N
1952	35	28	37	32	25	42	1,899
1956	31	34	35	24	30	46	1,762
1958	35	41	24	18	38	44	1,450
1960	31	36	33	23	30	47	1,181
1964	35	41	24	23	31	46	1,571
1968	33	37	30	39	29	33	1,557
1972	32	45	24	27	42	31	2,705
1976	35	45	20	24	42	34	2,248
1978	21	62	17	19	55	26	2,304
1980	25	52	23	21	47	32	1,614
1982	34	43	23	23	40	37	1,418
1984	26	49	25	19	49	32	2,257
1986	27	50	23	20	50	30	2,176
1988	26	44	29	23	42	36	2,040
1990	31	53	16	20	49	30	1,980
1992	36	45	19	22	43	35	2,485
1994	27	44	29	33	41	26	1,795

Differences Between the Major Parties

5. NES: Do you think that there are any important differences in what the Republicans and Democrats stand for?

	1986%	1988%	1990%	1992%	1994
No difference	44	35	46	35	41
Yes, a difference	48	60	48	60	52
DK	9	6	6	5	5
N	1,079	1,773	976	2,250	1,787

6. Roper: Some people say there are real differences between the Democratic and Republican Parties in terms of what the parties believe in and stand for.

Others disagree. Which one of the statements on this card best expresses how you feel about the differences between the two major political parties?

	1/78 (%)	1/84 (%)
The Republican Party and the Democratic Party are quite different and stand for quite different things.	18	25
While the differences between the Republican Party and the Democratic Party aren't that great, there are still some basic differences between them.	41	42
There really is no difference between the two parties themselves, only between individuals within the parties.	35	27
DK	6	6
N	2,002	2,000

7. ABC/WP: (I'm going to read a few statements. For each can you please tell me if you tend to agree or disagree with it, or if, perhaps, you have no opinion about the statement?) . . . The two political parties do more to confuse the issues than to provide a clear choice on issues.

	10/81 (%)	7/83 (%)	2/85 (%)
Agree	66	65	64
Disagree	24	31	25
DK/no opinion	10	4	10
N	1,512	2,530	1,506

Performance of Two-Party System

8. LAT: Do you think the two-party system in this country is basically sound or unsound?

	9/95 (%)	10/95 (%)
Sound	58	47
Unsound	38	49
DK	4	4
N	1,152	1,426

Support for a New, Third Party

9. Roper, CNN/USA: What parties would you like to see competing in the next presidential race (election) . . . Republican and Democrat only . . . Republican and Democrat and minor parties as before . . . Republican, Democrat, and a new strong third party . . . two new parties with all conservatives and all liberals voting together?

	Roper 5/38 (%)	CNN/USA[a] 9/95 (%)
Republican and Democrat only/Republican, Democrat, and minor parties as before/continuing two-party system	65	26
Republican, Democrat, and a strong new third party/creating a new independent party that would exist along with other parties	13	53
Two new parties with all conservatives and all liberals voting together/creating a party that would replace the (Republican/Democratic) party	6	12
DK	15	7
None, other (volunteered), depends	. . .	3
	5,151	640

[a]Which of the following situations do you think would be best for the country . . . continuing the two-party system as it is, with just the Republican and Democratic Parties, creating a new independent party which would exist along with the Republican and Democratic Parties, creating a new independent party which would replace the Republican Party, or creating a new independent party that would replace the Democratic Party?

10. Roper, Gallup, USORC, CNN/USA: On the whole, how do you feel about the present set-up of the political parties here in the United States—Do you find that you are usually satisfied with the stands taken by one or the other of the present big parties, or would you like to see a strong new party entirely different from either of the present parties?

[TABULAR DATA OMITTED]

11. Gallup, Harris: Suppose a new party were to be organized in the U.S.—to be called the Center Party and represent Republicans and Democrats alike who would like a middle-of-the-road administration. Do you think the Center Party would be a good idea or a poor idea?

	Gallup 11/65 (%)	Gallup[a] 10/78 (%)	Gallup[a] 6/79 (%)	Harris[b] 11/83 (%)
Yes, agree	23	41	37	39
No, disagree	54	42	48	57
No opinion	24	17	15	4
N	1,646	1,543	1,511	1,252

[a]It has been suggested that the nation needs a new party—one that appeals to people who are middle-of-the-road in their political views. If there were such a party, then the Republicans would represent the people on the right, the conservatives; the Democrats would represent the people on the left, the liberals; and the new party would represent those in between or in the middle. Do you think there is or is not a place for such a Center Party in the United States today?
[b]For most of our history, the U.S. has had a two-party political system, under which most elections are won by either the Democratic or Republican Party. Let me read you some statements about the two-party system and suggestions that have been made to set up a major new third party. For each tell me whether you agree or disagree with the statement. . . . Neither the Republicans nor the Democrats stand for things I can go along with, and it is time to have a reasonable mainstream alternative in a new third party.

12. ABC/WP, T-M: Tell me if you tend to agree or disagree with [the following statement], or if perhaps, you have no opinion about the statement— We should have a third major political party in this country in addition to the Democrats and Republicans.

[TABULAR DATA OMITTED]

13. CBS/NYT: Some people say that the country needs a new political party to compete with the Democratic and Republican Parties in offering the best candidates for political office. Do you agree or disagree?

	6/92 (%)	11/94 (%)	3/95 (%)	8/95 (%)	11/95 (%)	12/95 (%)	4/96[a] (%)
Agree	58	57	53	55	51	57	53
Disagree	36	39	41	39	43	37	42
DK/N.A.	6	4	6	6	6	6	5
N	1,315	1,429	1,023	1,478	744	1,111	1,257

[a]Some people say the country needs a third political party—a new party to compete with the Democratic and Republican Parties. Do you agree or disagree?

14. Time/CNN: Would you favor or oppose the formation of a third political party that would run candidates for president, Congress, and state office against the Republican and Democratic candidates?

	6/3-4/92 (%)	10/92 (%)	6/93 (%)	1/94 (%)	8/94 (%)	3/95 (%)
Favor	58	63	50	54	59	56
Oppose	32	28	37	35	32	34
Not sure	10	9	13	11	9	10
N	1,200	1,653	901	1,000	1,000	1,010

15. ABC/WP, WP: Would you support or oppose the formation of a third political party that would run candidates for president, Congress, and state offices against Democratic and Republican Party candidates? (If support or oppose, ask:) Do you feel that way strongly or only somewhat?

	ABC/WP 9/95 (%)	WP 10/95 (%)
Support strongly	31	25
Support somewhat	31	38
Oppose somewhat	14	16
Oppose strongly	19	16
No opinion	5	6
N	1,530	839

Support for Specific Third Party Presidential Candidates, 1948–1992

16. Gallup: If a presidential election were being held today, and Harry Truman were running for president on the Democratic Party ticket

against Thomas Dewey on the Republican Party ticket and against Henry Wallace on a third party ticket, how would you vote?

[TABULAR DATA OMITTED]

Support for Colin Powell as an Independent Candidate

17. Time/CNN, NBC/WSJ, CBS/NYT, CNN/USA, ABC/WP, Newsweek: Suppose the 1996 election for president were being held today, and you had to choose between Bill Clinton, the Democrat; Robert Dole, the Republican; and Colin Powell, running as an independent. For whom would you vote—Clinton, Dole, or Powell?

[TABULAR DATA OMITTED]

New Party versus Elections without Party Labels

18. Harris, NES: Which of the following would you prefer? (Choose only one.)

	Harris 7/92 (%)	NES1993 Pilot (%)	NES 1994 (%)
A continuation of the two-party system of Democrats and Republicans	29	30	39
Elections in which candidates run as individuals without party labels	38	31	37
The growth of one or more new parties that could effectively challenge the Democrats and Republicans	30	36	23
Not sure	2	3	2
N	1,256	632	1,770

Desire for More Independent Candidates

19. Roper: (A number of people have said they would like to see changes in the kind of people who are elected to public office. Here is a card that has a number of the kinds of changes that ought to be made. For each pair on that list, would you indicate the direction you would like to see us move, as far as political officeholders are concerned?)

	9/74 (%)	9/78 (%)	9/86 (%)
More independent candidates	60	59	54
More party candidates	23	26	27
DK	17	15	19
N	1,998	2,002	1,997

Feeling Thermometers: Independents, Third Parties

20. NES, Greenberg: I'd like to get your feelings toward some of our
    political leaders and other people who have been in the news. I'll read
    the name of a person and I'd like you to rate that person using
    something called the feeling thermometer. You can choose any number
    between 0 and 100. The higher the number, the warmer or more
    favorable you feel toward that person; the lower the number, the
    colder or less favorable. You would rate the person at the 50 degree mark if
    you feel neither warm nor cold toward them. If we come to a person
    whose name you don't recognize, you don't need to rate that person.

    Just tell me and we'll move on to the next one. . . . . How would you
    rate the following . . . people who call themselves independents?

	NES 1980 (%)	NES 1982 (%)	NES 1984 (%)	Greenberg[a] 11/94 (%)
Positive, warm	34	33	25	31
Neutral	36	35	46	. . .
Negative, cool	18	19	20	36
Never heard of, no opinion, DK	12	14	10	33[b]
N	1,614	1,418	2,257	1,250

[a]Now I'd like to rate your feelings toward some people and organizations, with 100 meaning a very warm, favorable feeling, zero meaning a very cold, unfavorable feeling, and 50 not particularly warm or cold. You can use any number from zero to 100; the higher the number, the more favorable your feelings are toward that person or organization. . . . An independent, third political party?
[b]Includes neutral.

Colin Powell as an Independent versus as a Party Candidate

21. Time/CNN: If (Colin) Powell were to run for president in 1996, would
    you prefer that he ran as a Democrat, Republican, or independent?

	6/95 (%)	9/95[a] (%)	10/95[a] (%)
Democrat	17	2[b]	. . .
Republican	22	31	30
Independent	40	45	47
Other (volunteered)	2	4	. . .
Not sure	19	18	23
N	1,000	1,000	951

[a]If (Colin) Powell were to run for president in 1996, would you prefer that he run as a Republican or an independent?
[b]Volunteered.

Support for an Unspecified Third Party Candidate

22. NBC/WSJ: If there were a significant third political party established for the
    1996 presidential election, separate from the Republican and Democratic

Parties, how likely would you be to support its candidate: extremely likely, quite likely, somewhat likely, just a little likely, or not likely.

	10/14–18/94 (%)	9/16–19/95[a] (%)
Extremely likely, almost certain	6	5
Quite likely, very likely	8	7
Somewhat likely, about 50-50	29	37
Just a little likely, less than 50-50	12	12
Not likely	27	20
Depends (volunteered)	16	16
Not sure	2	3
N	1,509	1,005

[a]Same question as above, but response categories changed to almost certain, very likely, about 50-50, less than 50-50, or not likely.

Importance of Having a Major Party President

23. Newsweek, CNN/USA, Gallup: Some people feel that only a Democratic or Republican president can govern effectively because he can depend on the support of his party. Others feel that any strong candidate with good leadership skills could be a good president. How important do you think it is for the president to be from one of the two major parties? Would you say very important, somewhat important, not too important, or not at all important?

[TABULAR DATA OMITTED]

CRITICAL THINKING QUESTIONS

1. In what ways were Ross Perot's presidential ambitions both a cause and a consequence of public discontent with the two major parties?

2. How has support for the two-party system changed over time? How does this affect the potential for a viable third party?

3. What do the polls cited indicate about the public's opinion regarding the ability of a third party to govern? How would this likely affect the electoral fortunes of third parties?

4. This article was published in 1996. How might the 2000 presidential election have altered how people feel about third parties?

REFERENCES

Abramson, Paul R., John H. Aldrich, Phil Paolino, and David W. Rohde. 1995. "Third Party and Independent Candidates: Wallace, Anderson, and Perot." *Political Science Quarterly* 110:349–67.

Beck, Paul Allen. 1984. "The Dealignment Era in America." In *Electoral Change in Advanced Industrial Democracies: Realignment or Dealignment,* ed. Russell J. Dalton, Scott C. Flanagan, and Paul Allen Beck. Princeton, NJ: Princeton University Press.

Black, Gordon S., and Benjamin D. Black. 1994. *The Politics of American Discontent.* New York: Wiley.

Broder, David S. 1971. *The Party's Over.* New York: Harper & Row.

Dennis, Jack. 1975. "Trends in Public Support for the American Party System." *British Journal of Political Science* 5:187–230.

Herrnson, Paul S. 1994. "The Revitalization of the National Party Organizations." In *The Parties Respond: Changes in American Parties and Campaigns,* 2d ed., ed. L. Sandy Maisel. Boulder, CO: Westview.

Keith, Bruce E., David B. Magleby, Candice J. Nelson, Elizabeth Orr, Mark C. Westlye, and Raymond E. Wolfinger. 1992. *The Myth of the Independent Voter.* Berkeley and Los Angeles: University of California Press.

Lowi, Thoeodore J. 1994. "Toward a Responsible Three-Party System." In *The State of the Parties: The Changing Role of Contemporary American Parties,* ed. Daniel M. Shea and John C. Green. Lanham, MD: Rowman & Littlefield.

Nie, Norman H., Sidney Verba, and John R. Petrocik. 1979. *The Changing American Voter,* enlarged ed. Cambridge, MA: Harvard University Press.

Reichley, A. James. 1994. "The Future of the American Two-Party System." In *The State of the Parties: The Changing Role of Contemporary American Parties,* ed. Daniel M. Shea and John C. Green. Lanham, MD: Rowman & Littlefield.

Rosenstone, Steven J., Roy L. Behr, and Edward H. Lazarus. 1984. *Third Parties in America: Citizen Response to Major Party Failure.* Princeton, NJ: Princeton University Press.

Wattenberg, Martin. 1996. *The Decline of American Political Parties, 1952–1994.* Cambridge, MA: Harvard University Press.

9

Campaigns and Elections

Unrecorded Votes and Election Reform

David C. Kimball, Chris T. Owens, and Katherine McAndrew Keeney

Roughly 2 million voters (almost one in every 50 to cast a ballot) failed to record a choice for president in the 2000 elections. These unrecorded votes are the result of "undervotes" (where voters make no selection) and "overvotes" (where too many selections are recorded). In Florida, more than 175,000 ballots failed to record a vote for president (mostly overvotes).

Several election reforms have been proposed to reduce the number unrecorded votes.[1] Many of the reform proposals focus heavily on voting equipment. However, in the current economic climate state and local governments may be unwilling to spend a lot of money on new voting equipment even if some federal funding is available. Election laws and administrative decisions that determine ballot design strongly influence the number of unrecorded votes and are less expensive to change than voting technology. By focusing so much attention on voting technology, the election reform movement may be missing other cost-effective methods to reduce the number of unrecorded votes in future elections.

Spectrum: the Journal of State Government, Wntr 2003, v76, i1, p34(4).

© 2003 Council of State Governments.

A BRIEF EXAMINATION OF THE 2000
PRESIDENTIAL ELECTION

We start by examining unrecorded votes in 2895 American counties in the 2000 election. While this sample covers 92 percent of all counties and 95 percent of votes cast for president in the 2000 election, we could not get complete data for every county. Not all states require local election officials to count or report the number of unrecorded votes or the total number of ballots cast in an election. In addition, a few jurisdictions reported erroneous totals (as when the number of presidential votes exceeds the number of ballots cast). Thus, a basic element of any election reform proposal should require local election administrators to count and report the number of overvotes, undervotes, and ballots cast, in addition to the vote totals for each candidate in every election.

Among the counties in our sample, over 1.8 million unrecorded votes were cast m the presidential contest (1.8 percent of ballots cast). In one out of every four counties, more than 3 percent of the ballots failed to record a vote for president. It is important to keep in mind that unrecorded votes can occur because of overvotes (selecting too many candidates) and undervotes (not recording a choice for any candidate). Overvotes are almost certainly the result of voter error (perhaps due to confusion with voting equipment, ballot instructions, or ballot design). In contrast, undervotes may be the result of voter confusion (e.g., people may fail to cast a proper vote if they do not understand the voting procedure) or the voter's intent to abstain if none of the candidates are appealing. Thus, there are multiple causes of the high number of ballots with unrecorded votes in the United States.

There are six basic methods of voting in the United States: paper ballots, lever machines, Votomatic punch card machines, Datavote punch cards, optical scan ballots and direct recording electronic (DRE) machines. DRE machines and optical scan systems are the newest technologies, seeing increased use as jurisdictions replace older methods (paper ballots, lever machines and punch cards). Optical scan systems can also be divided into those where ballots are counted at a central location (like the county courthouse) or at the voting precinct. One advantage of the precinct-count optical scan systems is that they give voters a chance to discover and correct possible mistakes (overvotes and undervotes). The central-count optical scan systems do not have such an error-correction feature. Finally, a small number of counties (almost entirely in states where elections are administered by townships) use more than one type of voting technology.

Votomatic punch card machines (source of the infamous "hanging chad") produce the highest rate of unrecorded votes (at least one percent higher than any other voting method).[2] After the Votomatic, however, differences between other voting methods in terms of unrecorded votes are not as large. In comparing newer technologies, precinct-based optical scan systems performed better than central-count optical scan systems and electronic machines in 2000. Among the newer voting methods, only the precinct based optical scan system performed significantly better than lever machines and paper ballots. Thus, if

**Table 1. Unrecorded Votes in the 2000 Presidential Election
by Voting Equipment**

Voting Technology	Description
Punch Card—Votomatic (505 counties, 28% of ballots)	Punch card is inserted behind booklet with ballot choices voter uses stylus to punch out holes in card. Ballots counted by card reader machine.
Optical Scan-Central Count (838 counties, 15% of ballots)	Voter darkens an oval or arrow next to chosen candidate on paper ballot. Ballots counted by computer scanner at a central location.
Electronic (DRE) (310 counties, 11% of ballots)	No ballot. Candidates are listed on a computerized screen—voter pushes button ortouches screen next to chosen candidate. DRE machine records and counts votes.
Lever Machine (372 counties, 15% of ballots)	No ballot. Candidates are listed next to levers on a machine—voter pulls down the lever next to chosen candidate. Lever machine records and counts votes.
Paper Ballot (260 counties, 1% of ballots)	Candidates are listed on a sheet of paper—voter marks box next to chosen candidate. Ballots counted by hand.
Punch Card—Datavote (44 counties, 3% of ballots)	Ballot choices are printed on punch card—voter punches out hole next to chosen candidate. Ballots counted by card reader machine.
Mixed (59 counties, 6% of ballots)	More than one voting method used.
Optical Scan-Precinct Count (507 counties, 20% of ballots)	Voter darkens an oval or arrow next to chosen candidate on paper ballot. Ballots counted by computer scanner at the precinct, allowing voter to identify and fix mistakes.

Voting Technology	Unrecorded Votes
Punch Card—Votomatic (505 counties, 28% of ballots)	2.80%
Optical Scan-Central Count (838 counties, 15% of ballots)	1.80%
Electronic (DRE) (310 counties, 11% of ballots)	1.70%
Lever Machine (372 counties, 15% of ballots)	1.60%
Paper Ballot (260 counties, 1% of ballots)	1.60%
Punch Card—Datavote (44 counties, 3% of ballots)	1.20%
Mixed (59 counties, 6% of ballots)	1.10%
Optical Scan-Precinct Count (507 counties, 20% of ballots)	1.90%

the overall frequency of unrecorded votes is the main concern of election administrators, counties using lever machines, paper ballots, or Datavote punch cards may not need to rush to buy new voting equipment unless they can afford a precinct-count optical scan system.

If confusion is a cause of unrecorded votes, then ballot features that make it easier for voters to complete a ballot may reduce the number of unrecorded votes. One such feature is the straight-party option, which appeared on the presidential ballot in 15 states in the 2000 election. The straight-party option, which typically appears at the top of the ballot with each parry's name and logo, allows people to cast a vote for the same parry in every contest on the ballot. Our analysis reveals that the straight-party ballot device reduces the number of unrecorded votes. In states with a straight-party option on the ballot, 1.3 percent of the ballots cast failed to record a vote for president in 2000. By comparison, in states without straight-parry voting, 2.0 percent of ballots failed to record a vote for president.[3] Aside from replacing Votomatic machines with any other voting method, the impact of the straight-party option on un-recorded votes appears to be larger than a change in voting equipment. This evidence is consistent with other studies showing that unrecorded votes are less common when the ballot design minimizes voter confusion.[4]

Furthermore, the straight-party option reduces the socio-economic disparity in unrecorded votes. Ballots with unrecorded votes are more common in counties or precincts with large populations of racial and ethnic minorities, low-income residents, less-educated residents or elderly voters.[5] However, this familiar pat-tern is largely absent in states with straight-party voting (see Table 2).

Table 2. Racial and Economic Disparity in Unrecorded Votes

Unrecorded votes in states with no straight-party voting

RACIAL COMPOSITION OF COUNTY	
Less than 10% black	1.50%
Between 10% and 30% black	2.30%
Over 30% black	3.70%
MEDIAN INCOME OF COUNTY	
Less than $25,000	4.40%
Between $25,000 and $32,500	2.60%
Between $32,500 and $40,000	2.30%
Over $40,000	1.30%
RACIAL COMPOSITION OF COUNTY	
Less than 10% black	1.40%
Between 10% and 30% black	1.10%
Over 30% black	1.30%
MEDIAN INCOME OF COUNTY	
Less than $25,000	2.00%
Between $25,000 and $32,500	1.50%
Between $32,500 and $40,000	1.50%
Over $40,000	1.10%

Some studies indicate that the elevated rate of unrecorded votes associated with confusing ballots and voting technology falls disproportionately on racial and ethnic minorities and the poor.[6] It appears that disadvantaged groups are more confused by certain voting methods. We find that DRE voting machines, lever machines and precinct-based optical scan systems reduce the racial and economic disparity in unrecorded votes. These voting methods have features that help prevent voting mistakes. For example, when programmed properly, electronic machines and lever machines do not allow voters to cast votes for more than one candidate. Other voting methods do not have these same features and thus exacerbate socio-economic differences in unrecorded votes.

SOME UNRECORDED VOTES
ARE INTENTIONAL

The straight-party option is not the only ballot characteristic that influences unrecorded votes. It may be that some voters intentionally leave the ballot blank if they do not like any of the listed candidates. For example, there was a substantially higher rate of unrecorded votes in the seven states where Ralph Nader was left off the ballot (2.8 percent). In the 24 states including Nader on the ballot, the number of unrecorded votes was 1.7 percent. This suggests that voters who preferred Nader may have abstained from the presidential contest if his name was not on the ballot.

Of course, a write-in vote is an alternative for voters who want to register disapproval of the available choices on the ballot; however, many states severely limit write-in voting. Ten states simply did not include space on the ballot for write-in votes in the 2000 presidential election. Another 25 states allowed write-in votes but only counted write-ins cast for candidates who had filed a declaration of candidacy. Thus, some voters in these states made write-in selections that were not counted as valid votes. In states that restricted write-in voting, 2.0 percent of the ballots failed to record a vote for president in 2000. In the 14 states that counted all write-in votes for president, only 1.1 percent of the ballots failed to record a vote for president. Finally, Nevada deserves mention as the only state to include a ballot line for "None of These Candidates" in federal and statewide races. Only 0.6 percent of the ballots in Nevada failed to record a vote for president (one of the lowest rates in the country).

Thus, national data indicate that changes in voting technology (replacing Votomatic punch card voting machines) and ballot design (including straight-party and write-in options) would reduce unrecorded votes. While the national data give an indication of the sources of unrecorded votes, the main controversy over uncounted ballots focused on the state of Florida.

WHAT HAPPENED IN FLORIDA?

The 2000 presidential election in Florida produced a "perfect storm" in terms of unrecorded votes. Florida ranks above the national average in its population of low-income residents, non-white residents, and elderly residents, all factors associated with higher levels of unrecorded votes. At the same time, Florida does not have a straight-party option on the ballot and the state only counts write-in votes for declared candidates. Furthermore, the largest counties in Florida used Votomatic punch cards in the 2000 election. To top it all off, 10 presidential candidates qualified for the Florida ballot in 2000, prompting several counties to list presidential candidates in multiple columns or pages, creating further confusion for some voters. The combination of all of these forces produced over 175,000 unrecorded votes for president (roughly 2.9 percent of ballots cast in Florida), one of the highest rates in the country.

We examined a database of unrecorded votes in the 2000 presidential election (including overvotes and undervotes) from each Florida voting precinct (gathered by a consortium of newspapers and provided by USA Today).[7] Roughly 65 percent of the unrecorded votes for president in Florida were overvotes, a higher share of overvotes than in other states that reported such data. This suggests that voter confusion was a major source of unrecorded votes in the Florida election.

While punch card ballots contributed to the large number of unrecorded votes in Florida, ballot design was the most critical source of unrecorded votes in the state. Because of a change in state law that eased ballot access requirements for minor parties, ten presidential candidates qualified for the ballot in Florida (a high number compared to other states). Nineteen counties in Florida listed the presidential candidates in more than one column.

Listing presidential candidates in two columns had important consequences. In counties where candidates were listed in one column, 2.1 percent of the ballots contained unrecorded votes for president. In counties where candidates were listed in more than one column, unrecorded votes for president jumped to 7.6 percent of ballots cast.[8] Some voters mistakenly thought that each new column represented a new contest, and they overvoted by selecting a candidate from each column. Overvotes were much more common in counties with the confusing two-column ballot design (5.9 percent of ballots cast as compared to 1.2 percent where candidates were listed in one column).

As in the national data, we also find an interaction between ballot design and race and income. In Florida counties with the confusing presidential ballot design, high rates of overvotes and unrecorded votes were concentrated in precincts with large black or low-income populations. Indicates, in counties that adopted the confusing ballot design, well over one of every 10 voters in heavily poor or black precincts mistakenly voted for more than one presidential candidate. In contrast, in counties that listed presidential candidates in a single column, overvotes remained below 4 percent even in precincts with the largest populations of poor or black residents.

These results raise concerns about unequal treatment and representation of voters in American elections, especially in light of the "equal protection" rationale used by the Supreme Court to decide the 2000 presidential election in the *Bush v. Gore* case. Changes in ballot features and the replacement of Votomatic punch cards will help reduce the disparate impact of unrecorded votes in future elections. In addition, improved poll worker training and voter education efforts (especially in areas with concentrated low-income and minority populations) are worth pursuing.

CONCLUSION

Ballot design and voting methods influence the frequency as well as the racial and economic distribution of unrecorded votes. While voters probably intend some unrecorded votes, it is clear that many unrecorded votes are the product of confusion and mistakes by voters.

In the wake of the 2000 elections, many counties are considering new voting technology, and there is intense competition between manufacturers of electronic voting machines and optical scan systems to replace older voting methods. In some quarters, optical scan voting methods are touted as the best available equipment in terms of minimizing the number of unrecorded votes.[9] This recommendation may need to be qualified, particularly since the central-count optical scan systems appear to perform no better than any alternatives to punch cards. If one is interested in reducing the disproportionate racial and economic impact of unrecorded votes, our evidence suggests that precinct-count optical scan systems and electronic voting machines perform better than central-count optical scan methods.

Furthermore, in the march to election reform it is important to look beyond voting technology. Switching to a new voting technology can be very costly, while relatively inexpensive changes in ballot design may have a bigger effect in reducing the number of unrecorded votes in future elections. Adding ballot lines (such as the straight-party and write-in options) that help voters complete an error-free ballot and avoiding designs that create confusion (like listing candidates for the same office in multiple columns or pages) may go a long way toward minimizing the number of unrecorded votes, at least in high-profile contests that appear near the top of the ballot.

David C. Kimball is assistant professor of political science at the University of Missouri—St. Louis. His research focuses on voting, interest groups and election reform.

Chris T. Owens is a doctoral student in political science at Texas A&M University. His research focuses on political participation, election reform and minority politics.

Katherine McAndrew Keeney is a Master's student in political science at Southern Illinois University at Carbondale. Her research interests and prior work experience include campaigns and elections and electoral behavior.

ENDNOTES

1. To read many of the election reform proposals, see the web site maintained by the Election Reform Information Project at http://www.electionline.org/news.jsp?s=reports.

2. For more detailed research on unrecorded votes in the 2000 presidential election, see Jonathan N. Wand, Kenneth W. Shotts, Jasjeet S. Sekhon, Walter R. Mebane, Jr., Michael C. Herron, and Henry E. Brady., "The Butterfly Did it: The Aberrant Vote for Buchanan in Palm Beach County, Florida," *American Political Science Review* 95 (2001): 793–810; David C. Kimball, Chris Owens, and Katherine McAndrew, "Who's Afraid of an Undervote?" (paper presented at the annual meeting of the Southern Political Science Association, Atlanta, November 9, 2001); Caltech/MIT Voting Technology Project, Voting: What Is, What Could Be, July, 2001 (http://www.vote.caltech.edu/Reports/index.html; Minority Staff, Special Investigations Division, Committee on Government Reform, U.S. House of Representatives, "Income and Racial Disparities in the Undercount in the 2000 Presidential Election" (July 9, 2001: http://www.house.gov/reform/min/pdfs/pdf_inves/pdf_elec_nat_study.pdf); United States General Accounting Office, Elections: Statistical Analysis of Factors That Affected Uncounted Votes in the 2000 Presidential Election (GAO-02-122, October, 2001, http://www.gao.gov/); Henry E. Brady, Justin Buchler, Matt Jarvis, and John McNulty, *Counting All The Votes: The Performance of Voting Technology in the United States* (Survey Research Center and Institute of Governmental Studies, University of California, Berkeley, September, 2001, http://ucdata.berkeley.edu/new_web/countingallthevotes.pdf).

3. These differences in rates of unrecorded votes remain statistically significant in a multivariate analysis that controls for voting technology and several demographic and election administration factors. See Kimball, Owens, and McAndrew, "Who's Afraid of an Undervote?"

4. Wand, et al., "The Butterfly Did it: The Aberrant Vote for Buchanan in Palm Beach County, Florida"; Robert Darcy and Anne Schneider, "Confusing Ballots, Roll-Off, and The Black Vote," *Western Political Quarterly* 42 (1989): pp. 347–364; Dennis Cauchon, "Errors Mostly Tied to Ballots, Not Machines," *USA Today* (November 7, 2001): p. 6A.

5. Jack L. Walker, "Ballot Forms and Voter Fatigue: An Analysis of the Office Block and Party Column Ballots," *Midwest Journal of Political Science* 10 (1966): pp. 448–464; James M. Vanderleeuw and Richard Engstrom, "Race, Referendums, and Roll-Off," *Journal of Politics* 49 (1987): pp. 1081–1092; Darcy and Schneider, "Confusing Ballots, Roll-Off, and the Black Vote;" Bullock and Dunn, "Election Roll-off: A Test of Three Theories;" Nichols and Strizek, "Electronic Voting Machines and Ballot Roll-Off;" Stephen M. Nichols, "State Referendum Voting, Ballot

Roll-off, and the Effect of New Electoral Technology," *State and Local Government Review* 30 (1998): pp. 106–117; Brady, et al. Counting All The Votes: The Performance of Voting Technology in the United States; United States General Accounting Office, Elections: Statistical Analysis of Factors That Affected Uncounted Votes in the 2000 Presidential Election, GAO-02-122 (October, 2001) <http://www.gao.gov/>; Michael C. Herron and Jasjeet S. Sekhon, "Overvoting and Representation: An Examination of Overvoted Presidential Ballots in Broward and Miami-Dade Counties," *Electoral Studies* 22(2003): pp. 21–47; Stephen Knack and Martha Kropf, "Voided Ballots in the 1996 Presidential Election: A County-Level Analysis," *Journal of Politics*, forthcoming.

6. Darcy and Schneider, "Confusing Ballots, Roll-Off, and The Black Vote;" Knack and Kropf, "Invalidated Ballots in the 1996 Presidential Election: A County-Level Analysis;" Tomz and Van Houweling, "How Does Voting Equipment Affect the Racial Gap in Voided Ballots?."

7. We downloaded the Florida precinct data November 7, 2001, from http://www.usatoday.com/news/politics/nov01/ballots-usat.htm. The precinct figures compiled by the newspaper consortium did not include data for Glades County. There also was a disparity between official election results and the newspaper data for Martin County (the newspaper data indicated no unrecorded votes in the county). Thus, Glades and Martin counties are excluded from our analysis.

8. In a multivariate analysis of unrecorded votes in Florida that controlled for a host of demographic and election administration factors, the 2-column ballot design was the biggest source of unrecorded votes. Results are available from the authors. Also see Dennis Cauchon, "Errors Mostly Tied to Ballots, not Machines," *USA Today* (November 7, 2001), p. 6A.

9. Caltech/MIT Voting Technology Project, Voting: What Is, What Could Be: pp. 21–22; Caltech/MIT Voting Technology Project, "Residual Votes Attributable to Technology: An Assessment of the Reliability of Existing Voting Equipment."

CRITICAL THINKING QUESTIONS

1. What are the overall statistics regarding unrecorded votes in the 2000 presidential election?

2. What are the different types of unrecorded votes?

3. In what instances are unrecorded votes an intention of the voter?

4. What were the specifics of unrecorded votes and their impact in the 2000 Florida presidential election?

5. What are the most important reforms that could reduce the problem of unrecorded votes? Which do you think would be the most effective, and why?

10

The Congress

The Senate and Executive Branch Appointments

Burdett Loomis

AN OBSTACLE COURSE ON CAPITOL HILL?

"When you draw a line here and say, 'no further,' then you've basically
stopped the work of the Senate. It isn't a threat. It's a reality."

SENATOR LARRY CRAIG, REPUBLICAN POLICY
COMMITTEE CHAIR, JUNE 2000

Bolstered by analyses from both journalists and academics, the conventional wisdom now holds that the Senate has become increasingly hostile to presidential appointees. Would-be judges, justices, ambassadors,
commissioners, and executive branch officials are "borked" by vicious special
interests and their Capitol Hill co-conspirators. Appointees are "held hostage"
by senators who seek substantive trade-offs or the confirmation of their own
favored candidates for judicial or regulatory posts. Senators place so-called
"holds" on nominations, thus delaying matters interminably. All in all, the
Senate's performance, at least as commonly portrayed, does little to enhance
the appointment-confirmation process. Quite the contrary. The Senate, to re-
call Robert Bendiner's description of more than 30 years ago, seems a major
culprit in the lengthy and often distasteful politics of confirmation—a verita-
ble "obstacle course on Capitol Hill."

Brookings Review, Spring 2001, v19, i2, p32.

© 2001 Brookings Institution. Reprinted with permission.

This characterization fits with our broader understanding of the Senate of the past 20 years. As detailed by political scientist Barbara Sinclair and her fellow congressional scholars, the Senate has become both highly individualized and extremely partisan. At first blush, such a pairing seems unlikely—would not senators in a highly partisan legislature subordinate their individual desires for the good of the entire partisan caucus? But the Senate, once a bastion of collegiality, has become less civil, less cordial—sometimes almost rivaling the raucous House of the 1990s in its testiness. The lengthy, increasingly bitter partisan stand-off over the final year of the Clinton administration has given further credence to the perception that the Senate has become deeply hostile to appointments from a Democratic executive.

Still, headlines, assumptions, and conventional wisdom can be wrong, to a greater or lesser extent. We might do well to examine the data on confirmations. Do Senate confirmations take longer than they used to, especially in the modern era? Are more nominations withdrawn or returned to the executive?

Second, we might well ask how Senate processes might be altered in a partisan, individualistic era, especially when the upper chamber, unlike the rule-dominated House, usually operates through the mechanism of unanimous consent—that is, a single senator's objection can delay, if not stop, the normal legislative process. Even if we find that the conventional wisdom is accurate and that presidential appointments often run into a congressional roadblock, there may be little that can be done within the legislative branch. Indeed, Christopher Deering's assessment of Senate confirmation politics, circa 1986, bears repeating: "The relationship between the executive and legislative branches . . . remains essentially political. . . . The Senate's role in the review of executive personnel is but one example of that relationship. The Senate's role in the confirmation process was designed not to eliminate politics but to make possible the use of politics as a safeguard . . . a protection against tyranny." Circa the year 2000, one might well argue that more is going on than "protection against tyranny," but exactly what remains open to question.

The following discussion focuses on 329 top policymaking, full-time positions in the 14 executive departments that require presidential appointment and the approval of the Senate. Ambassadors, regulatory commission slots, military commissions, and federal attorneys are excluded.

EXECUTIVE BRANCH APPOINTMENTS
AND THE SENATE, 1981–99

To understand the magnitude of any "problem" with Senate confirmations of executive branch appointments, we need to know three things. First, how lengthy is the Senate confirmation process, and to what extent do some appointments take a disproportionately long time to be resolved? Second, how many appointments are withdrawn and returned? And third, how are appointments processed under differing conditions, such as divided government and various periods of a presidency (especially during the transition to a new administration as opposed to the remainder of a president's tenure)? Because the available data do not allow for systematic explorations before the Reagan administration, over-time comparisons are limited. Still, some trends do begin to emerge.

First, the confirmation process has grown longer. In 1981, the Republican Senate took an average of 30 days to confirm Ronald Reagan's executive branch appointees; in 1993, the Democratic Senate took 41 days to confirm Bill Clinton's first nominees, an increase of 37 percent. Six years later, in the first session of the 106th Congress, the confirmation process had dragged out to 87 days, more than twice the 1993 figure and almost three times that of 1981. The comparisons are skewed somewhat by the Republican control of the Senate in 1999 and the less urgent, less visible nature of confirming appointees late in an administration, as opposed to the initial round of appointments that receive considerable attention given the need to put a government in place a few weeks after the November election.

Still, the process has grown longer, both early and late in an administration. In 1992, for example, a sample of George Bush's appointments during the last year of his presidency (and facing a Democratic Senate) averaged 60 days for confirmation, in contrast to Clinton's 86 days in 1999 and early 2000. Thus the typical 1999 confirmation process averaged almost three months when Congress was in session. Taking into account the 34 days of late-summer congressional recess, the confirmation process of 1999 averaged 121 days—almost exactly four months. The positions, of course, did not necessarily remain vacant, because the 1998 Federal Vacancies Reform Act allowed acting officials to fill many slots. Still, the lengthening Senate confirmation process indicates that a problem does exist—all the more so given the increasing time that the president has taken to make appointments.

A second data set relates to the likelihood that a president's appointments will be confirmed. How often does the Senate return appointments to the president or cause nominations to be withdrawn? Again, looking at the rates under differing circumstances makes sense. The president is likely to do better with appointments he makes right after being elected than with any other, and divided government may affect confirmation rates.

As reported in table 1, Presidents Reagan, Bush, and Clinton fared about the same in winning confirmation for their nominees. All three won approval of more than 95 percent of their appointees in their administrations' first two years, but did less well for the rest of their tenure in office. To the extent that a trend emerges, it reinforces the inference that the Senate has put up more obstacles over time. Reagan's nominees were confirmed at an 86 percent clip between 1983 and 1988, whereas Clinton won approval for only 79 percent of his appointments. But Clinton faced a Republican Senate for the entire six-year stretch, while Reagan dealt with a Democratic chamber only in his last two years, when his confirmation rate fell to 82.5 percent (much like Bush's 81.6 percent success rate in 1991–92, under similar conditions).

A summary view of confirmations over the past two decades demonstrates that the Senate process has grown longer, that divided government lowers

Table 1. Confirmed, Returned, and Withdrawn Executive-Branch Nominees, 1981–99

Years	Nominees	Confirmed		Returned	
		Number	(Percent)	Number	(Percent)
Bill Clinton					
1999	85	68	(80.0)	0	
1997–98	207(**)	166	(80.2)	16	(7.8)
1995–96	79	59	(74.7)	19	(24.1)
1993–94	323	310	(96.0)	9	(2.8)
George Bush					
1991–92	136	111	(81.6)	21	(15.4)
1989–90	292	278	(95.5)	8	(2.7)
Ronald Reagan					
1987–88	159	131	(82.5)	24	(15.1)
1985–86	182	165	(90.7)	14	(7.7)
1983–84	111	93	(83.8)	18	(16.2)
1981–82	269	260	(96.7)	6	(2.2)

Years	Withdrawn(*)	
	(Percent)	Number
Bill Clinton		
1999	3	(3.5)
1997–98	9	(4.3)
1995–96	1	(1.7)
1993–94	4	(1.2)
George Bush		
1991–92	4	(2.9)
1989–90	0	
Ronald Reagan		
1987–88	4 (2.5)	
1985–86	3	(1.7)
1983–84	0	
1981–82	3	(1.1)

(*) In 1999, 14 appointments were carried over; in 1998, 9 recess appointments were made
(**) Included 16 carryover appointments

Source: Various Congressional Research Service studies, 1983–2000, compiled by Rogelio Garcia.

confirmation rates a bit, and that the president's capacity to win Senate approval for his nominees declines modestly. At the same time, President Clinton did win confirmation of 96 percent of his nominees in the first two years of his administration, albeit with less dispatch than did Ronald Reagan in 1981.

This leads us to consider whether the Senate is truly the culprit here and, if it is, whether anything might be done to affect the way the chamber handles the confirmation process.

THE SENATE: PARTISAN, INDIVIDUALISTIC, AND SEPARATE

Aside from anecdotal evidence of particular bitter confirmation fights, such as former Senator John Tower's failure to win confirmation as secretary of defense in 1989, or ineptly handled appointments, such as Lani Guinier and Zoe Baird in the Clinton transition, we have little systematic data on how the Senate affects confirmation politics in the post-1980 era of increased individualism and stronger partisanship. Nevertheless, convincing evidence does exist that the Senate has become both more individualistic and more partisan. Barbara Sinclair, for example, reports steady growth in filibusters over the past 40 years, especially in the past 20, and Sarah Binder and Steven Smith demonstrate that the use of filibusters continues to reflect the policy goals of individual senators, groups of senators, and, at times, the minority party. Moreover, the Senate continues to consider itself a co-equal partner within the appointment process. As separation-of-powers scholar Louis Fisher observes, "The mere fact that the President submits a name for consideration does not obligate the Senate to act promptly." Indeed, the Senate's willingness to sit on a nomination may reflect its status in a "separate-but-equal" system.

Still, the unlikely combination of individualism and partisanship surely defines the contemporary Senate. As Sinclair summarizes, by the mid-1970s, the Senate "had become a body in which every member regardless of seniority considered himself entitled to participate on any issue that interested him for either constituency or policy reasons. Senators took for granted that they—and their colleagues—would regularly exploit the powers the Senate rules gave them." Senators also emphasized "their links with interest groups, policy communities and the media more than their ties with each other." And, notes Sinclair, by the late 1980s, "Senators were increasingly voting along partisan lines. In the late 1960s and early 1970s, only about a third of Senate roll call votes pitted a majority of Democrats against a majority of Republicans. By the 1990s, from half to two-thirds of roll calls were such party votes. . . . By the 1990s a typical party vote saw well over 80 percent of the Democrats voting together on one side and well over 80 percent of the Republicans on the other." In fact, in the 105th Congress, Senate party loyalty scores slightly exceeded those of the House, which has been seen as the more partisan chamber.

Unsurprisingly, the heightened individualism and partisanship has affected the confirmation of executive branch nominees. Guarantees by the Senate leadership to the contrary, every senator can place a "hold" on a nomination—delaying it, if not delivering a death sentence—though this tactic has been used more visibly on ambassadorial than on executive department appointments.

Even noncontroversial nominations can fall victim to highly partisan Senate politics, as nominees are "held hostage" to other nominations, to appropriations bills, or to substantive legislation. Where there is real controversy, as with the appointment of Bill Lann Lee to head the Justice Department's civil rights division, partisan conflict increases and extends beyond Congress to the Senate's relationship with the White House.

CONFIRMATION AND THE SENATE

The great majority of presidential appointees to high-level executive positions win approval by the Senate, although the success rate hovers at about 80 percent once a president has initially constructed his administration. Adding to their uncertainty, these later appointees must wait an average of four months for the Senate to act, once it has received their nomination. For these nominees, the process is long, and the outcome uncertain. Add to this the partisan politicking and the intense scrutiny, and it is no wonder that some potential officeholders decline the honor of nomination.

Might the Senate smooth the way for future nominees? Given the profound changes in the chamber over the past 25 years—the great latitude allowed individual members and the intense partisanship that dominates much decision making—it seems unlikely that reformers would profit much from attempting to reshape Senate procedures. The best circumstance for speedier and more successful confirmations would be for the same party to control both the Senate and the presidency. Ronald Reagan did better in the mid-1980s with a Republican Senate than did either George Bush or Bill Clinton with opposing-party control in the 1990s. Bridging the separate institutions may be more valuable than seeking to reform an institution that has proven highly resistant to planned change.

Burdett Loomis is professor of political science and program coordinator at the Robert Dole Institute for Public Service and Public Policy at the University of Kansas.

CRITICAL THINKING QUESTIONS

1. What helps explain why there has been increased opposition to presidential appointments in recent years?
2. How long does the typical confirmation process take? What is a typical probability of success?
3. Why might some people decline a position that requires Senate confirmation?
4. Why is it easier for presidential nominations to gain swift approval when the presidency and the Senate are controlled by the same party?

11

The Presidency

War Powers: A New Chapter
Continuing Debate

Charles F. Williams

B ecause the Constitution gives Congress—and not the president—the
power "to declare war," public debate arises every time the president
leads the nation into war without bothering to seek such a declaration.

That leads to a lot of debates, because Congress has formally declared war
in only five conflicts (the War of 1812, the Mexican War, the Spanish-American
War, World War I, and World War II) while U.S. presidents have committed
armed forces to more than one hundred combat operations around the world
in addition to full-fledged, undeclared wars in Korea, Vietnam, the Persian
Gulf, and the former Yugoslavia.

For the past thirty years, the so-called War Powers Act, 50 U.S.C. §
1541–1548, has also been in the picture, although just barely. A joint resolution
passed over President Nixon's veto in 1973, the act was explicitly meant to
limit the president's war-making powers. Its purpose is bluntly stated: To "insure
that the collective judgement of both the Congress and the President will
apply to the introduction of United States Armed Forces into hostilities."

The act's requirements are equally specific. The president can commit
U.S. troops to war only if there is either specific statutory authority for such
actions, a declaration of war, or a national emergency created by an attack
on the United States. He or she must consult with Congress "in every possible instance" before introducing U.S. armed forces into war. He or she

Social Education, April 2003, v67, i3, p128(4).

© 2003 National Council for the Social Studies.

must report any military commitment to Congress within forty-eight hours and must continue to report on the status of the conflict no "less often than once every six months." Perhaps most importantly, unless Congress authorizes continuing commitment, troops must be withdrawn after sixty to ninety days.

WAR POWERS IN PRACTICE

The two salient facts about the War Powers Act are, first, that it is clear and unambiguous, and second, that since its passage, no president has ever admitted to being bound by it.

As John Dean, President Nixon's White House Counsel put it, presidents will sometimes decide, for political reasons, to report to Congress "consistent with" the resolution, but none has ever reported "pursuant to it." (1)

Although Congress passed the War Powers Resolution in the belief that it would cause presidents to seek Congress's advice and approval, the resolution's ninety-day limit has never been applied, and every president has asserted his constitutional authority as commander in chief to unilaterally order troops into battle.

Although, according to the Congressional Research Service, by the end of 2002 presidents had submitted ninety-nine reports to Congress as a result of the resolution (2), each has appeared to interpret the act's requirement that he "consult with" Congress to mean that he must simply "inform" it after a planned action is already underway.

As President Ford, who was sworn in as president upon Nixon's resignation, put it:

> The United States was involved in six military crises during my
> 30 months as president: the evacuation of US citizens and refugees from
> Da Nang, Phnom Penh and Saigon in the spring of 1975; the rescue of
> the Mayaguez in May 1975; and two evacuation operations in Lebanon
> in June of 1976.
>
> In none of these instances did I believe the War Powers Resolution
> applied. Many members of Congress also questioned its applicability in
> cases involving protection and evacuation of American citizens. Further-
> more, I did not concede that the resolution itself was equally binding or
> legally binding on the president on constitutional grounds. Nevertheless,
> in each instance, I took note of its consultation in reporting provisions
> and provided certain information on operations and strategies to key
> members of the House as well as the Senate. (3)

Deputy Assistant Attorney General John C. Yoo in his April 17, 2002, Senate testimony on applying the War Powers Resolution to the War on

Terrorism, cited other modern presidential decisions to commence major military operations including:

- President Harry Truman: Did not seek congressional authorization, but relied instead on his "inherent executive and commander-in-chief powers" to commit the United States to the Korean War.

- President John F. Kennedy: Claimed constitutional authority to act alone in deploying a U.S. naval quarantine around Cuba in response to the Cuban Missile Crisis.

- President Lyndon B. Johnson: While the Gulf of Tonkin Resolution, 78 Stat. 384, expressed some level of congressional support for military intervention, he insisted that "as commander in chief the responsibility is mine and mine alone" to order military actions in Southeast Asia.

- President George H. W. Bush: Declared that he had the constitutional authority to unilaterally initiate war, and committed five-hundred thousand soldiers to warfare in Operation Desert Storm for a period of time that violated the War Powers Resolution.

- President William Clinton: Did not seek congressional permission before sending the military into action in Somalia, Haiti, Bosnia, the Middle East, and Kosovo. Clinton's assistant secretary of state, Barbara Larkin, testified before Congress that "this administration, like previous administrations, takes the view that the President has broad authority as Commander-in-Chief . . . to conduct foreign relations, to authorize the use of force in the national interest."

Thus, Yoo testified, the reality is that "The President has taken the primary role in deciding when and how to initiate hostilities. Congress has allowed the executive branch to assume the leadership and initiative in war, and instead has assumed the role of approving military actions after the fact by declarations of support and by appropriations." (4)

For students accustomed to thinking of a textbook government of checks and balances and neat divisions of power, such an outcome can be baffling. If the Constitution says Congress shall declare war, why doesn't it? If the War Powers Act says presidents may conduct war only pursuant to the act, why don't they?

WAR POWERS IN THEORY

As noted, the Constitution itself divides war-making powers between Congress and the president. Specifically, according to Article I, Section 8, Clause 1, Congress has the power to declare war, raise and support armies, call forth the militia to execute U.S. laws, suppress insurrections, and repel invasions. The president's authority to act as commander-in-chief of the armed forces is spelled out in Article II, Section 2, Clause 1.

There have been—and perhaps always will be—at least two viewpoints regarding how the executive and legislative branches should work together during the days leading up to and following the decision to go to war. Under one theory pressed by supporters of a strong congressional role, the founders envisioned a system whereby only after Congress decided to go to war would the president, as commander-in-chief, have the authority to lead the nation against the enemy designated by Congress.

That was the argument raised by the plaintiffs in Doe v. Bush and Rumsfeld, decided March 13, 2003, by the U.S. Court of Appeals for the First Circuit.

The plaintiffs—including six Democratic members of the House of Representatives and a number of soldiers and parents of military personnel—sought to enjoin President George W. Bush from launching military operations against Iraq without first obtaining congressional authorization.

Their lawsuit noted that the resolution on Iraq that Congress passed on October 16, 2002 (House Joint Resolution 114) did not declare war, but simply authorized the president to:

> use the Armed Forces of the United States as he determines to be necessary and appropriate in order to defend the national security of the United States against the continuing threat posed by Iraq; and enforce all relevant United Nations Security Council resolutions regarding Iraq. (5)

That broad authorization, the Doe plaintiffs said, amounts to an unlawful ceding of the congressional war-making decision to the president.

The district court disagreed, concluding that the issues raised by the plaintiffs involved "political questions," which are beyond the authority of a federal court to resolve. "As a general proposition," U.S. District Judge Joseph Tauro wrote in dismissing the suit, it is the responsibility of the "political branches" of government—the legislative and executive—to conduct foreign policy. Usually, "the judiciary has no role to play." (6)

Could the courts ever get involved? Yes. For example, Tauro wrote:

> [S]hould it become apparent that the political branches, themselves, are clearly and resolutely in opposition as to the military policy to be followed by the United States, then the situation would have gone beyond that of a political question and would pose a serious constitutional issue requiring resolution by the judicial branch. And so, a federal court may judge the war policies of the political branches only when the actions taken by Congress and those taken by the Executive manifest clear, resolute conflict. (7)

Nevertheless, he concluded, "Congress does not have the exclusive right to determine whether or not the United States will engage in war. Congressional ratification for the continuation of undeclared war activity may be found even though there has not been a formal declaration of approval. The manner and form of ratification is up to Congress, and the courts have no power to second guess the wisdom or form of such approval."

It turns out that that reasoning is precisely the theory most often pressed by those in favor of allowing greater presidential power in war-making decisions.

The founders, these executive-branch boosters say, "did not understand the Constitution to establish a precise, permanent process for making war in the same manner that it created a detailed method for making laws." (8)

Under this view, the framers deliberately avoided making a clear statement about the consequences of giving Congress "the power" to declare war. They did not, for example, draft anything along the lines of "the president shall not, without consent of Congress, engage in war." By opting instead for the more ambiguous Article I clause, they sought to ensure "a fluid and flexible system that could expand and change to meet international challenges, and that could recede and change shape during more quiescent periods." (9)

In upholding the district court's ruling, the court of appeals also stressed this point, reasoning that while Congress has not formally declared war against Iraq, there is no merit to:

> the formalistic notion that Congress only authorizes military deployments if it states, "We declare war." This has never been the practice and it was not the understanding of the founders. See J.H. Ely, *War and Responsibility* 25–26 (1993).
>
> Congressional authorization for military action has often been found in the passage of resolutions that lacked these "magic words," or in continued enactments of appropriations or extensions of the draft that were aimed at waging a particular war. (10)

Moreover, said the First Circuit, there is no "clear evidence" that Congress has abandoned its authority.

> [C]ourts are rightly hesitant to second-guess the form or means by which the coequal political branches choose to exercise their textually committed constitutional powers. As the circumstances presented here do not warrant judicial intervention, the appropriate recourse for those who oppose war with Iraq lies with the political branches. (11)

PAST AND FUTURE

The arguments on both sides of this constitutional debate have a distinguished pedigree. As already noted, presidential proponents can point to the wartime behavior of any number of commanders in chief throughout American history who felt unconstrained by either the Declare War Clause or, in recent times, the War Powers Act.

Critics of this presidential power can point to historical figures as well.

Northeastern University School of Law Professor Margaret Burnham, a coauthor of the plaintiffs' brief in Doe v. Bush, cites Thomas Jefferson for his observation that the intent of the Declare War Clause was to restrain the "Dog of War" by "transferring the power of letting him loose from the Executive to the Legislative . . . " (12)

Veteran New York Times reporter Tom Wicker shares the sentiment but prefers Abraham Lincoln, who he quotes as writing the following:

> Allow the President to invade a neighboring nation, whenever he shall deem it necessary to repel an invasion, and you allow him to do so whenever he may choose to say he deems it necessary for such purpose—and you allow him to make war at pleasure. Study to see if you can fix any limit to his power in this respect. . . . If, today, he should choose to say he thinks it necessary to invade Canada, to prevent the British from invading us, how could you stop him? You may say to him, "I see no probability of the British invading us" but he will say to you, "Be silent, I see it, if you don't." (13)

As long as the courts permit Congress to declare war without using the "magic" words that make it clear that it knows that declaring war is exactly what it is doing, however, there is no reason to think it will stop embracing the ambiguity that allows it to take credit for participating in wars that prove popular while distancing itself from any war that takes a bad turn. And as long as Congress stops short of clear and forthright opposition to a president's actions as commander in chief, he or she will be able to assert even greater power.

One serious, real-world check on the presidency, however, always remains, for wars are expensive and only Congress can pay for them. That is to say, as Yoo testified at last year's Senate hearing, that although the president has the power of the sword, "Congress has the power of the purse." And if the president has virtually unfettered discretion to commit military forces to battle, it also remains true that he commands "only those military forces which Congress has provided." (14)

Charles F. Williams is editor of Preview of United States Supreme Court Cases, a publication of the American Bar Association in Chicago, Illinois.

NOTES

1. John Dean, "Findlaw Forum: President Needs Congressional Approval to Declare War on Iraq," CNN.COM Law Center (August 30, 2002) available at www.cnn.com/2002/LAW/ 08/columns/fl.dean.warpowers

2. Richard F. Grimmett, "War Powers Resolution: Presidential Compliance," CRS Reports (September 30, 2002) available at www.iraqresearch.com/html/ib81050a.html

3. Gerald R. Ford, "The War Powers Resolution," Alfred M. Landon Lecture on Public Issues (Monday, February 20, 1978) available at www.ford.utexas.edu/library/speeches/780220.htm

4. John C. Yoo, "Applying the War Powers Resolution to the War on Terrorism," 6 Green Bag 2nd 175 (Winter 2003) available from Lexis-Nexis.

5. H.J.Res. 114 (October 16, 2002) available at www.house.gov/becerra/IRAQ_resolution.pdf

6. Doe I et al. v. Bush and Rumsfeld No. 03-10284-JLT (Mem. Op. Feb. 24, 2003).

7. Ibid.

8. John C. Yoo, "CLIO at War: The Misuse of History in the War Powers Debate," 70 U. Colo. L. Rev. 1169, 1172 (Fall 1999) available at www.law.berkeley.edu/faculty/yooj/articles/clio.htm

9. Ibid., 1219.

10. Doe v. Bush, No. 03-1266 (1st Cir., March 13, 2003)

11. Ibid.

12. Margaret Burnham, "War Powers: Towards Unchecked Executive Authority?" *Jurist* (February 25, 2003) available at jurist.law.pitt.edu/Forum/Forumnew99.php

13. Tom Wicker, "Press Isn't Asking Right Questions About Iraq," *Editor and Publisher Online* (March 11, 2003) available at www.editorandpublisher.com

14. John C. Yoo, "Applying the War Powers Resolution to the War on Terrorism," 6 Green Bag 2nd 175 (Winter 2003) available from Lexis-Nexis.

CRITICAL THINKING QUESTIONS

1. What are the two factors, which characterize the use of the War Powers Act since 1973?

2. What other ways can Congress control the President's commander-in-chief powers?

12

The Bureaucracy

The Human Side of Public Administration

Louis C. Gawthrop

To avoid any misunderstanding, let me say at the outset that the remarks that follow are selective impressions brimming with bias, the product of what one of our earlier distinguished colleagues, George Graham, described as old-fashioned armchair research. To talk about the human side of public administration is a good opening salvo designed to attract attention, but what I really want to focus my comments on is a thread that is woven deeply within the fibers of administration, and that now, more than ever before, needs to be brought to the surface and recognized explicitly as an integral aspect of our democratic heritage. Specifically, I am referring to the humanistic imperatives that democracy historically weaves into the fabric of public administration.

The fascinating thing about history is the never-ending flow of irony that fills its pages. This is particularly true insofar as the primary focus of this lecture, presented in honor of one of our most distinguished former colleagues, John Gaus, is concerned. For example, as Dwight Waldo noted some years ago, "there is an intricate and intimate relationship between civilization and administration. . . . Administration was present 'at the creation.' It was an integral part of civilization whenever and wherever civilization developed; and without the foundation and framework it supplied, civilization would not have developed" (1980, 17, 24–25).

PS: Political Science & Politics, Dec 1998, v31, i4, p763(7).

"The human side of public administration," by Louis Gawthrop. Reprinted with permission of Cambridge University Press.

Indeed, civilization and administration are virtually indivisible. In the earliest records of the most primitive and elementary social systems, there is evidence of decisions being made and implemented concerning issues of governance, however that term may have been defined. As the notion of governance was developed and extended, the expanse and influence of administrative systems grew. With the steady amplification of rudimentary social systems into increasingly elaborate systems of governance, the notions of politics and political systems became increasingly linked with the concept of a public administration designed to implement the policy decisions of ruling regimes or governments. Thus, it is in this context that the aphorism "politics is the lifeblood of administration" takes on a distinctive meaning, and the relationship between politics and administration becomes just as intricate and intimate as that between civilization and administration.

As Waldo (1980) pointed out, this ever-widening, dynamic development of an administrative presence began in the earliest of the ancient civilizations and continues to the present day. Yet—and here is where the irony occurs—for all intents and purposes, the development of public administration in the United States has been essentially a twentieth-century phenomenon. To be sure, administration was present at the creation of the Republic, as well as throughout the nineteenth century as Leonard White (1943, 1951, 1954, 1958) comprehensively recorded for us in his four-volume administrative history. In so many very important respects, however, the mature elements of the public sector administrative systems in the United States did not become fully developed until the late-nineteenth and early-twentieth centuries. In this regard, I am thinking primarily in terms of

1. The development of a self-conscious sense of professionalism
2. The development of public administration as a field deserving serious scholarly study
3. The explicit disciplinary commitment to the formation of a science of administration
4. The persistent emphasis placed on the politics–administration and fact–value dichotomies, and the emergence of well-defined perspectives concerning the validity of these presumed dichotomies
5. The continuous efforts to resolve the clash between the values of democracy and the canons of management.

Of course, many of my colleagues date the beginnings of modern public administration in the United States to 1933, which marks the beginning of the New Deal and the emergence of the positive state. In this connection, the British political scientist Harold Laski observed

As soon as the American democracy moved into the epoch of the positive state, it could not afford the luxury of dull government. For it is an inherent implication of dull government that the dynamic of national life is *not* profoundly affected by its operation; and it is to the inherent dynamic of the positive state that the operations of government *are* profoundly important.

From this it follows that the government of a positive state—if it is to be successful—must necessarily be a *thinking* government. (1940, 270–71; emphasis added)

A similar note was struck by Felix Frankfurter in his 1930 book on administration and democracy, *The Public and its Government*. Frankfurter drew on the traditions of public service in Great Britain and cited an 1854 report on civil service reform authored by Sir Charles Trevelyan. The "Organization Report," as it was referred to, anticipated very closely the conclusion reached by Laski, in the sense that the report

was based throughout upon the *positive idea of government*—that is, upon the idea that government must be carried on by men who think as to what ought to be done instead of merely doing that which must be done. (Frankfurter 1930, 141; emphasis added)

Gaus and the other distinguished political scientists of his generation viewed administration as an integral component of such a "thinking" government and, even more, as the impetus for nurturing and nourishing a thinking democratic polity. Gaus understood the role of the citizen to be that of a direct participant in the processes of democracy and this was especially true insofar as the role of the citizen in the administrative process was concerned (1947, 122). With the emergence of the positive state, Gaus argued, a healthy and satisfactory life for the individual could be obtained only through varied and extensive political arrangements, and these arrangements were largely administrative in nature. Thus, reciprocal relationships had to be developed between administrative officials and the citizenry to facilitate the exchange of information and to enhance the qualitative levels of a thinking government. As Gaus noted, "Some have called this kind of political society 'the service state' or 'the administrative state'. . . . whatever term we may give it, administration ultimately is *education*" (123; emphasis added).

This is an interesting proposition and, although it may sound somewhat like a quaint and prosaic soundbite to our more sophisticated and jaundiced ears, it does seem to suggest that the operations of a positive or thinking government rely upon ongoing public education, the responsibility for which falls primarily on the shoulders of administrative personnel. As another distinguished political scientist, Marshall Dimock, argued in this connection, "*administration is more than a lifeless pawn. It plans, it contrives, it philosophizes, it educates,* it builds for the community as a whole" (Gaus, White, and Dimock 1936, 133; emphasis added). In other words, in the context of a positive, policy-oriented state, administration becomes the primary service-delivery system for democracy and, in effect, the principal manager of democracy's end products. In regard to the delivery of tangible goods and things, this understanding of administration has become commonplace today. Our colleagues of nearly sixty years ago, however, seemed to be urging something quite different. They seemed to be suggesting that the basic end product of government is its capacity to educate, that is to say to inform, to impart knowledge, to increase citizen comprehension of (and appreciation for) the humanistic imperatives of democracy.

In my recent writing (Gawthrop 1998), I have focused extensively on the relationship between democracy and public service and specifically on the informational (or educational, if you will) relationships that must prevail among public servants and the citizenry if the basic democratic values of freedom, equality, justice, and responsibility are to be realized. Such a position does not seem too far removed from that taken by Gaus and his distinguished contemporaries who argued that an informed and "thinking" body politic could be realized only through the concerted efforts of the principal delivery system of government. From their perspective, and mine, the primary "thing" to be delivered by the administrative system is education designed to enhance the qualitative well-being of the citizenry by constantly integrating the fundamental humanistic imperatives of democracy into a viable and dynamic sense of community, civility, and the common good.

In other words, the responsibilities for involving citizens in the democratic processes of governance and developing in them an enriched sense of community, civility, and the common good, rest squarely on the shoulders of public administrators. Viewed from this perspective, democracy, at its best, takes the form of an ongoing pedagogical process that reflects something similar to the Platonic notion of an "intelligent love"—i.e., a type of love based on the notion of a transcendent good that, in turn, serves as a guide for action.

Such a love demands serious reflection and, of course, its true meaning is derived only when it is directed toward enhancing the well-being of another self. Its reality, in other words, is attained only through its relation and, as the American author, essayist, and critic Lionel Trilling has argued, "the deepest and truest relationship that can exist between human beings is pedagogic. This relationship consists in the giving and receiving of knowledge about right conduct, in the formation of one's character by another, and the acceptance of another's guidance in one's own growth" (1980, 77).

Following Laski, my argument to this point has been that the emergence of a positive state demands the development of a thinking government, and the primary component in such a democratic system must be a thinking administration. An essential element of such a proactive administrative system is a perspective that encourages one to view democracy as something more than a procedural set of mechanistic contrivances designed to maintain an orderly society. Just what that "something more than" is may have been best defined by John Dewey, the American philosopher and educator, in a lecture delivered over seventy years ago. According to Dewey, "Democracy is not an alternative to other principles of associated life. It is the idea of community life itself. It is an ideal in the only intelligible sense of an ideal: namely, the tendency and movement of something which exists carried to its final limit and viewed as completed, perfected" (1927, 148). Thus, democracy, perceived in terms of an idea and an ideal, created for Dewey a problem that was essentially a moral one, dependent upon the degree of intelligence and education utilized by the body politic. Democracy, Dewey observed, "is a name for a life of free and enriching communion" (184). It would seem to follow, then, that the realization of a free and enriching communion becomes a basic responsibility of a viable and dynamic administrative system committed to the humanistic imperative of an intelligent love. Certainly this attitude was clearly reflected in the writings of such scholars as Gaus, Dimock, Wallace Sayre, Paul Appleby, Charles Ascher, and Norton Long.

Each of these individuals moved directly, in his own particular fashion, to place administration in a more comprehensive setting with a clear normative emphasis on the integral relationships that must be forged among administrative practices and democratic values. As a consequence of these efforts, we are, today, once again confronted with assessing the role public administration is to play in the formation of democratic values among the body politic.

"The sense of the importance of values," Emmette Redford wrote in a 1950 issue of the *American Political Science Review*, "needs to pervade the study of administration" (283). Similarly, in a *Public Administration Review* article assessing the trends of administrative values during the 1940s, Wallace Sayre noted,

> Our values, in one context, have moved from a stress upon managerial techniques of organization and management to an emphasis upon the broad sweep of public policy—its formulation, its evolution, its execution, all either within or intimately related to the frame of administration. In another context, our values have moved away from the confining view of an "administrative man," responding mechanically to the imperatives of technological management, toward broader and deeper perspectives of human behavior in cooperative action. (1951, 4)

Other distinguished political scientists, such as Fritz Morstein Marx and Robert Dahl, also expressed their concerns about a value-free administrative system. "One is left with the suspicion that the purer a science of administration, the less will it be socially relevant," observed Morstein Marx. Moreover, according to Dahl, a non-normative science of public administration involved a basic hypothesis that was "loaded with enormous and perhaps insuperable difficulties" (quoted in Sayre 1951, 5).

Even such scholars as Herbert Simon, Donald Smithburg, and Victor Thompson, who were among the leaders of those who sought to develop a science of administration, stated in their classic text that their "emphasis on the factual does not mean that we discount the importance of values." Although the significance they assigned to values seems somewhat narrowly focused, the role of values in public administration, even from their scientific perspective, should not be ignored. "No knowledge of administrative techniques," they wrote, can relieve the administrator from the task of moral choice—choice as to organization goals and methods and choice as to his treatment of the other human beings in his organization. His code of ethics is as significant a part of his equipment as an administrator as is his knowledge of administrative behavior, and no amount of study of the "science" of administration will provide him with this code. (Simon, Smithburg, and Thompson 1950, 19–24)

Interestingly, the task of moral choice referred to by Simon, Smithburg, and Thompson can be viewed alternately in positive and negative terms. If the notion of moral choice is perceived in the more constricted sense of a clearly defined code of ethics, a negative morality is bound to prevail in a manner thoroughly consistent with the characteristics of a negative, reactive, detached state. To a very real extent, codes of ethics devised in this context become sets of procedural ethics as reflected in clearly defined rules, regulations, and procedures. On the other hand, if the notion of moral choice is seen as encompassing the fundamental humanistic values of democracy, then a positive sense of ethical/moral consciousness can be advanced as the basic responsibility of all public administrators to insure that every moral choice is specifically intended to enhance the well-being of the citizenry.

As one legal scholar has noted, "positive liberty is a fertile land, laden with promise" (Farina 1994, 100). Similarly, a positive sense of ethical/moral administrative consciousness that has at its core the humanistic values of democracy is also a fertile land, laden with promise. In a democratic framework, the effectiveness of a positive state that evolves from a thinking government must depend directly on the substantive and qualitative efficacy of a positive and dynamic administration. A positive administration of the sort Gaus and his colleagues advanced must reflect the highest levels of maturity, authenticity, sincerity, responsibility, and caring. Moreover, if administration's principal mission is educational, as Gaus argued, its most elevated manifestation of this mission must be revealed in its sensitivity toward the sanctity of democratic communion and community.

There is a difficulty, however, in developing a positive ethic for government that is grounded in the normative values of sincerity, authenticity, caring, communion, and covenant. For example, the British author, Graham Greene, wrote in one of his novels, "caring is the only dangerous thing" (Greene 1974, 271). Viewed from an organizational perspective, the consequences of being sincere, expressing genuine concern, or truly caring can be quite dysfunctional. The danger, of course, results from the personal commitment that an administrator would be required to make either to one's colleagues or to one's fellow citizens—i.e., their clients or "customers." Like the biblical mustard seed, the tiniest bit of a personal ethical-moral commitment can amplify dramatically into a complex reticulation. Elsewhere, Graham Greene quoted from Joseph Conrad: "I only know that he who forms a tie is lost. The germ of corruption has entered into his soul" (Greene 1979, 2). What is being referenced here is the sense of moral obligation that comes to dwell in one's conscience when a commitment is made to someone or some transcendent higher good. Such a sense of obligation runs counter to the rational decision making required to ensure the continued functioning of the complex macrosystems that comprise public sector organizations. It is for this reason, therefore, that one of the oldest traditions stemming from the most ancient civilizations is the concept of a detached and objective administrative impersonality.

In administering the Biblical Law, for example, the Pharisees were characterized by French philosopher Paul Ricoeur as revealing a scrupulous consciousness, "anxious to satisfy the law in all things, without making an exception of any sector of existence, without taking into account exterior obstacles . . . and which gives equal importance to little things as to great." It is the scrupulous person who encloses him or herself in the inextricable labyrinth of commandments, detached from any positive human relationship by the protective insulation of objective impersonality. In the process, however, Ricoeur reminds us that "obedience to a commandment because it is commanded becomes more important than love of neighbor or even love of God; this exactitude in observance is what we call legalism" (1971, 16).

Indeed, it is this expression of a negative, dispassionate morality that T.S. Eliot brought to life in the speech the Third Knight delivers directly to the audience after he and his colleagues have completed their murder in the cathedral.

> There is one thing I would like to say. . . . In what we have done, and whatever you may think of it, we have been perfectly disinterested. We are not getting anything out of this. We have much more to lose than to gain. We are just four plain Englishmen who put their country first. . . . So as I said at the beginning, please give us at least the credit for being completely disinterested in this business. (1938, 78–79)

This expression of negative morality is very similar to what I have described previously as an "ethics of civility" (Gawthrop 1984, 138) and to what Lionel Trilling referred to as a "morality of inertia" (1956). An ethics of civility can be viewed as a highly structured, mechanistic ethics that places democratic values primarily in a negative framework designed to insure scrupulous adherence to the law and the maintenance of order. Similarly, Trilling spoke of a morality of inertia that would seem to fit well in the overall context that Laski referred to as "dull" government, that is, negative, non-thinking government.

It is the dull, daily world of an unimaginative bureaucracy that Trilling saw as the primary source of moral inertia.

> It knows that duties are done for no other reason than they are said to be done; for no other reason, sometimes, than that the doer has not really been able to conceive of any other course—has, perhaps, been afraid to think of any other course. (1956, 44)

The pithy insight Rufus Miles passed on to us from his days in the Bureau of the Budget as a career public administrator—"Where you stand depends on where you sit" (1978)—could very easily be twisted out of context and turned into a clarion cry for moral inertia. Moral choice is not an option in an environment of moral inertia, as Trilling pointed out. Necessity alone dictates actions, a necessity the administrator can neither refuse or even imagine refusing. Imposed by circumstance and maintained by habit, moral inertia negates any connection between administrative actions and the purposefulness of democracy. Indeed, it negates any connection between the reality of the present and the hopes of the future. Such a morality animates deeds performed without thought and without choice, but also, most certainly, without excitement and without love, and without compassion—or, as Max Weber would say, *sine ira ac studio,* without anger or enthusiasm (1946, 216). As Trilling described it,

> The morality of inertia, of the dull, unthinking round of daily duties, may, and often does, yield the immorality of inertia. The example that will most readily occur to us is that of the good simple people, so true to their family responsibilities, who gave no thought to the concentration camps in whose shadows they lived. (1956, 46; see also Mankowski 1991, 85)

In his *Reflections on Public Administration,* John Gaus noted that "education viewed as a continuing process from youth to retirement . . . is decisive in its importance for instigating and supporting those inner controls which the individual, often alone on the firing line, must exercise in a world in which our very existence is dependent upon countless agents and deputies of the public" (1947, 119–20; emphasis added). As the United States enters the twenty-first century, the external controls over the government's administrative systems seem to be fairly well in place. The fundamental issue of the degree of discretion permitted public administrators is no longer any mystery. The legislative and judicial branches of government know what buttons to push to increase or decrease the level of administrative discretion permitted in the implementation of public policy. However, as far as the inner controls that Gaus referred to are concerned, the situation seems to be less certain and not as well understood.

Over the past 100 years, administrators, legislators, and judges have become expert in confronting virtually any problem situation in government and defining what can be done to resolve or dissolve the problem. Moreover, they have become equally expert in defining how to do it. They have largely failed, however, to answer, or, in most instances, even ask the question of why.

Without a clear perception of the moral purposefulness inherent in democracy, the why questions can never be answered and the "inner controls" so important to Gaus and his contemporaries can never be activated. One consequence of this basic lack of understanding is that many are quick to gloss over or dismiss the relevance of such notions as substantive due process when its counterpart, procedural due process, is so much more effective in determining the what and the how of the decision process. Moreover, many are quick to ignore the fundamental point made by Reinhold Niebuhr, the distinguished

American theologian, that "any justice which is only justice soon degenerates into something less than justice" (1932, 258). This is the inertia of morality that Trilling decried and it reflects the ethical vacuum that is reflected in one stanza from a poem by Dorothy Sayers:

By lavish and progressive measures Our neighbor's wants are all relieved; We are not called to share his pleasures, And in his grief we are not grieved. (1969, 7)

To a very real extent, the short-term future of public administration in the United States is being determined by the demand for "reinventing government" and "managing for results," as well as the requirements of the National Performance Review and the Government Performance and Results Act. Not unlike what occurred during the 1890s and the early decades of the twentieth century, the current trend seems focused on the separation of administration from politics, with the desired outcome being a reconfiguration or refitting of Woodrow Wilson's 1887 model in the garb of a twenty-first-century information-age wizard. As I have tried to indicate, however, if students of administration have learned nothing else since the publication of Wilson's quasi-manifesto (1887), they certainly have learned that the type of administration defined as public is not a field of business and is not—and, indeed, should not be—removed from the hurry and strife of politics. Quite to the contrary, the empirical evidence scholars have assiduously gathered over the years clearly confirms the propositions advanced by many who have spoken from this podium in the past: namely, administration and democracy are indivisible; administration is education; politics is the lifeblood of administration; administration is caring. The truth of the matter is that well before the distinguished management scholar Douglas McGregor (1960) wrote about the human side of enterprise, one of the major accomplishments of the New Deal was to articulate an explicit commitment to the human side of public administration.

To be sure, there have always been—and still are—powerful voices in academia, in government, and in society at large that raise strenuous objections to characterizing public administration in such humanistic terms. In the eyes of these critics, the appropriate role of administration in the United States' system of democratic governance should be projected in much more attenuated, constrained, and purely reactive terms. From this perspective, administration is seen as a mechanistic and instrumental system designed solely to implement the policy intentions of the elected representatives of the people in a dutifully subservient (i.e., value-free) manner.

Despite the persistence of efforts to attain a predominately value-free administrative system, most people, regardless of position, have come to accept the notion that every society, community, organization, and individual must be guided by some value vision, some center of worth, if civilization is to endure and cohere. To use the example of another ancient Jewish community, the Essenes (as opposed to the Pharisees), one rabbinical scholar has noted, "represent a value system that was quite positive. There was no contradiction between morality, ethics, mutual love, and the observance of Jewish law and ritual. To them it was a unity" (Baumgarten 1989, 8). The question that I pose today is "To what extent do the components of ethics, morality, love, and justice fit together to form the substantive focus of America's value vision of democracy and of the human side of public administration?" How we, as scholars and citizens, respond will be a measure of our professional worth, to be sure; but more importantly it will also be a measure of our human worth.

As the twenty-first century moves closer, those who work and study in the field of administration need to be mindful, as noted previously, of John Dewey's observation that democracy is a name for a life of a free and enriching sense of communion and community. To be sure, this is an interesting proposition to discuss in the abstract; but discussing democracy in the abstract is like casting an unmarked ballot. Democracy needs to be transformed into action. If politics truly is the lifeblood of administration, as Norton Long (1949, 257) argued many years ago, is it not reasonable to suggest that administration is the lifeblood of democracy?

Democracy can be transformed from an abstract concept to an empirical reality only to the extent that the humanistic values that underlie the notions of communion and community are made real by positive and dynamic administrative action. Moreover, such administrative action has to be purposefully focused. That is to say, the human side of public administration can be made visible only to the extent that the human values of democracy are made viable. Both requirements can only be met, however, if and when policy programs are implemented by an administrative cadre fully committed to the worthiness of human growth, the wholesomeness of human communities, and the holiness of human dignity. This is the essence of a "thinking" administration; one that is energized by the humanistic imperatives of democracy. Certainly this view of administration was shared by Gaus and his colleagues. More significantly, however, they intuitively understood—just as contemporary scholars must understand—that in attempting to define and describe the human side of administration, one must use one's own humanity as a means to understanding.

This point was emphasized very clearly in an address then-director general of the World Health Organization George Brock Chisholm gave when accepting the Kurt Lewin Award at the 1948 meetings of the American Psychological Association. "Our own personal responsibility to our fellow humans is clear," Chisholm declared.

> Whoever is reasonably informed in any aspect of human emotional-mental-social development, whoever can do something to clarify thinking even a little and very locally, whoever can help to remove a prejudice, soften a hate, increase the total of understanding and tolerance in the world, by that knowledge, training, insight, or ability is made responsible to do what he can in all possible places. Research is valuable but may remain sterile for long periods, and time is short. Erudite papers read to

technical gatherings and published in technical journals have their important place, but may be futile unless appropriate action follows. Responsibility of the informed and technically qualified is to all people, not just to the enlightened. (Quoted in Gaus 1950, 166)

Chisholm's remarks are obviously appropriate when related to the world's health professions. The commitments made by countless doctors, nurses, and medical technicians to improve the quality of life, even on the smallest scale and in the most remote villages prompted Jan Tinbergen, Nobel laureate in economics, the father of econometrics, and internationally recognized expert in developmental economics, to refer to these dedicated individuals as "barefoot doctors." At one point he wrote, "We have seen the rise of the 'barefoot doctors;' we now must encourage the rise of the 'barefoot experts'" (1976, 109). In this connection, Tinbergen was referring to the specialists in the various social sciences and to the necessity for them to become involved at the lowest levels of third world communities where their expertise could have a direct and immediate positive impact. "Not only must specialists advocate courses of action," Tinbergen argued, "they must also more fully commit themselves to development efforts. . . . Their commitment must be total, their allegiance to a problem or community, unstinting" (109). And in this respect, the similarity between Tinbergen's perspective and Gaus's point concerning the educational function of administration should not be overlooked. Both seem to conclude that the principal mission of administration is to expand the potential for human growth and to enhance the value of human worth.

Indeed, it would seem that this is what Chisholm meant when he noted that whoever is reasonably informed in any aspect of human development is responsible to do what he or she can in all possible places to amplify the quality of life. Moreover, this relationship between administrators and citizens involves, as Dewey noted, the free and enriching sharing of thoughts and feelings and, as Wallace Sayre observed, the persistent development of broader and deeper perspectives of human behavior in cooperative action. Viewed in this context, the pertinence of Trilling's comment that "the deepest and truest relationship that can exist between human beings is pedagogic" assumes added significance. The primary focus of administration in a democracy would clearly seem to be, as Gaus suggested, pedagogical. As a consequence, it logically follows that the essence of the human side of public administration as it relates to its citizen clientele is the reciprocal and open exchange of information about right conduct, about the formation of one's character by another, and about the willingness to accept another's guidance in one's own growth.

Democracy is American society's way of managing itself. Moreover, in any democracy worthy of its name, it should not be unreasonable for society to show sympathy and compassion for itself. The human face of democracy is revealed by the kindness, benevolence, unselfishness, and justice embedded in its values. The human side of administration is evidenced when it is acting to implement the values inherent in democracy.

I claim no originality in stating that the human side of administration is the human face of democracy. Indeed, this notion certainly seems to be embedded in the oath of the Athenian city-state. It also informed governmental actions in fourteenth-century Florence in the wake of the Black Death. According to medieval historian Marvin Becker, the Florentines made no distinction between their role in civic life and the ethos of caritas.

Efforts were made to authenticate new social values and formulate codes of behavior more relevant for individuals living in greater isolation. To modern scholars, the stress on charity and love might indeed look evasive until one realizes that they surfaced with compelling force. These virtues alone could foster the family, guard the city, and even enlarge a Florentine empire. . . .

Man's dignity did not reside in solitary experience or in strategic personal relationships. Neither pride of caste nor cultivation of autonomous feelings of selfhood were sufficient to endorse this dignitas; instead, man's consciousness of his solidarity with all men was quintessential. (1974, 196)

Moreover, on our own shores, slightly more than 300 years ago William Penn observed:

Government itself . . . [is] as capable of kindness, goodness, and charity as a more private society. They weakly err that think there is no other use of government than correction which is the coarsest part of it. Daily experience tells us that the care and regulation of many other affairs, more soft and daily necessary, make up much of the greater part of government. (Quoted in Ahlstrom 1975, 166)

The human side of administration is the human face of democracy whenever democracy and administration are fused to form a positive and dynamic holistic system. There is no necessity to reinvent this political fact of life. But as scholars and citizens, our indebtedness to John Gaus and his colleagues needs to be reasserted and reaffirmed from time to time if for no other reason than to remind ourselves that we must follow their lead and use the humanistic imperatives of democracy to guide the human side of public administration into the next century.

CRITICAL THINKING QUESTIONS

1. What is the author referring in the title of his article?
2. In what ways is public administration compatible with democracy?
3. Does democracy require humanistic public administration?

REFERENCES

Baumgarten, Rabbi Joseph M. 1989. "The Dead Sea Scrolls." *Baltimore Sun Sunday Magazine*, 8–10.

Becker, Marvin. 1974. "Aspects of Lay Piety in Early Renaissance Florence." In *The Pursuit of Holiness in Medieval and Renaissance Religion,* ed. Charles Trinkhaus and Heiko A. Oberman. Leiden: E.J. Brill.

Dewey, John. 1927. *The Public and Its Problems.* New York: Henry Holt.

Eliot, T.S. 1938. *Murder in the Cathedral.* London: Faber and Faber.

Frankfurter, Felix. 1930. *The Public and Its Government.* New Haven: Yale University Press.

Gaus, John M. 1947. *Reflections on Public Administration.* University, AL: University of Alabama Press.

———. 1950. "Trends in the Theory of Public Administration." *Public Administration Review* 10(Summer): 161–68.

———, Leonard White, and Marshall Dimock. 1936. *The Frontiers of Public Administration.* Chicago: University of Chicago Press.

Gawthrop, Louis C. 1984. *Public Sector Management, Systems, and Ethics.* Bloomington: Indiana University Press.

———. 1998. *Public Service and Democracy.* New York: Chatham House.

Greene, Graham. 1974. *The Honorary Consul.* New York: Pocket Books.

———. 1979. *The Human Factor.* New York: Avon Books.

Laski, Harold. 1940. *The American Presidency.* New York: Harper and Brothers.

Long, Norton. 1949. "Power and Administration." *Public Administration Review* 9(Autumn): 257–64.

Mankowski, Paul. 1991. "The Discreet Domesticity of Evil." *The Human Life Review* 17(Summer): 85–88.

Miles, Rufus. 1978. "The Origin and Meaning of Miles' Law." *Public Administration Review* 38(September/October): 399–403.

McGregor, Douglas. 1960. *The Human Side of Enterprise.* New York: McGraw Hill.

Niebuhr, Reinhold. 1932. *Moral Man and Immoral Society.* New York: Charles Scribner's Sons.

Redford, Emmette. 1950. "The Value of the Hoover Commission Reports to the Educator." *American Political Science Review* 44(June): 283–98.

Ricouer, Paul. 1971. "Guilt, Ethics, and Religion." In *Moral Evil under Challenge,* ed. Johannes Metz. New York: Herder and Herder.

Sayers, Dorothy. 1969. "For An Evening Service." *Christian Letters to a Post-Christian World.* Grand Rapids, MI: Wm. B. Eerdmans.

Sayre, Wallace. 1951. "The Trends of a Decade in Administrative Values." *Public Administration Review* 11(Winter): 1–9.

Simon, Herbert, Donald Smithburg, and Victor Thompson. 1950. *Public Administration.* New York: Knopf.

Trilling, Lionel. 1956. "The Morality of Inertia." In *Great Moral Dilemmas in Literature, Past and Present,* ed. Robert McIver. New York: Harper.

————. 1980. *Sincerity and Authenticity.* New York: Harcourt, Brace.

Waldo, Dwight. 1980. *The Enterprise of Public Administration.* Novalto, CA: Chandler and Sharp.

White, Leonard. 1948. *The Federalists.* New York: Macmillan.

————. 1951. *The Jeffersonians.* New York: Macmillan.

————. 1954. *The Jacksonians.* New York: Macmillan.

————. 1958. *The Republican Era.* New York: Macmillan.

Weber, Max. 1946. "Essay on Bureaucracy." In *From Max Weber: Essays in Sociology,* eds. H.H. Gerth and C. Wright Mills. New York: Oxford University Press.

Wilson, Woodrow. 1887. "The Study of Administration." *Political Science Quarterly* 2(June): 197–222.

13

The Judiciary

The Five Dumbest Supreme Court Decisions

Daniel Franklin

Nathan Goodman's truck was only eleven-and-a-half feet from the railroad tracks when he first saw the oncoming train. An overhanging tool shed had obstructed the view of the railroad tracks and although he slammed on his brakes, there was nothing he could do to prevent crashing into the train. Luckily, he was only injured.

It was 1927, and America was just beginning to realize, perhaps not as profoundly as Goodman, that the country was not designed for the automobile driver. Goodman sued the Baltimore & Ohio Railroad Company and won, but the railroad appealed the decision to the Supreme Court. Justice Oliver Wendell Holmes, writing for a unanimous Court, stated that to prevent circumstances when "the accidental feelings of the jury" could decide personal injury claims, the Court needed to establish a steadfast rule by which the lower courts could decide liability.

Neither the railroad company nor the train's engineer has any responsibility to warn oncoming drivers, Holmes wrote. Rather, the burden of safety depends entirely on the driver. After all, "he knows that he must stop for the train, not the train stop for him." Therefore, Holmes concluded, any driver approaching railroad tracks must stop his car, get out, and walk up and down the tracks to make certain no train is coming before he can go on his way.

It isn't often that it can be said that a unanimous Supreme Court got something 100 percent wrong, especially when the driving force behind the error

Washington Monthly, Oct 1994, v26, n10, p12(7).

© 1994 Washington Monthly Company.

was one of the greatest legal minds in this country's history. How could Holmes have been so backward and blind? It probably had something to do with the fact that the good Justice had never sat behind the wheel of a car. The plight of Goodman, a professional truck driver, could not have been more alien to him.

Holmes' decision was overturned seven years later. Nonetheless, it provides a textbook example of how smart justices can come up with dizzyingly dumb decisions. Take *Bradwell v. Illinois,* in 1873, when the Court ruled that the State of Illinois could bar women from becoming lawyers because, they reasoned, God made women inherently inferior; or *Dennis v. U.S.,* in 1950, in which Smith Act prosecutions of Communist party leaders were justified on the basis that the mere advocacy of Communist doctrine was a crime. And then, of course, there are the truly infamous: Dred Scott, which in the process of returning a freed slave to his owner the Court affirmed that slaves were in fact property; and *Plessy v. Ferguson,* which in 1896 affirmed segregation and facilitated Jim Crow's hold on the South for another two generations.

Even though these decisions have been overturned, the Court over the past 30 years has come up with some decisions worthy of their, to be kind, less-than-perfect predecessors. Here are a few inane decisions that are the law of the land and shape—for the worse—the way we live today.

BOWERS v. HARDWICK, 1986

Until the last minute, Justice Lewis Powell wasn't sure on which side he would vote. The case before the Court would decide whether Georgia's statute outlawing sodomy between consenting adults was unconstitutional. As the justices debated the case in conference, their opinions began to polarize and harden: Justices Burger, White, Rehnquist, and O'Connor found for Georgia, while Justices Marshall, Blackmun, Stevens, and Brennan voted to strike down the law. The vote was four to four. Powell, attempting to reconcile his respect for the right to privacy with an instinctive disgust with homosexuality, sat divided in his own mind.

Bowers v. Hardwick had begun rather innocently in the summer of 1982, when Michael Hardwick was cited for carrying an open beer bottle in public. Hardwick paid the fine, but it had not been processed before a police officer was sent to Hardwick's Atlanta home one morning to serve him a warrant. A friend of Hardwick's who had spent the night in the house let the officer in and pointed him in the direction of Hardwick's bedroom. When the officer opened the door, he saw Hardwick engaged in oral sex with another man. The officer arrested both men on the charge of sodomy, a prohibition not enforced since 1935, and brought them to the police station.

Hardwick's attorney argued that the case presented a right to privacy issue: that the choice of whom to have sex with was something beyond the state's jurisdiction. Georgia Attorney General Michael Bowers (he still holds the position) countered by arguing that the right to privacy is not guaranteed in the Constitution and that the Supreme Court would be inventing a right (as many argued it did in *Roe v. Wade*) by asserting that there was a constitutional right to homosexual sex.

Powell, who tried desperately to find some middle ground, first voted against the Georgia law, but eventually added his name to the majority opinion written by Byron White.

White's opinion is a paradigm of bluster and bigotry. It argued that homosexuality was a historical taboo, and its inherent immorality made it vulnerable to the state's prohibition. Burger's concurring opinion was even more strident: Antisodomy laws have "ancient roots," he wrote, dating back to the Bible and the Roman Empire (both of which, he must have known, also condoned slavery and burning witches). Referring to Blackstone's commentary on English law, he described homosexuality as "the infamous crime against nature' as an offense of 'deeper malignity' than rape, a heinous act 'the very mention of which is a disgrace to human nature.'" In conclusion, he argued that protecting sodomy "would be to cast aside millennia of moral teaching."

It is a sad postscript to Bowers that Powell admitted after his retirement from the Court in 1987 that he had been wrong. During a 1990 appearance at New York University Law School, a student asked Powell to justify his vote on the case. Almost dismissively, he said, "I think I probably made a mistake in that one."

BUCKLEY v. VALEO, 1976

The commune depicted in George Orwell's *Animal Farm* is founded on one commandment: "All animals are created equal." But the pigs, who fancy themselves the ruling species, tack on an amendment: "But some animals are more equal than others." Similar to the animals in Orwell's classic, every American citizen has the freedom of speech. But some pigs, Ross Perot and Michael Huffington among them, have a little more freedom than the rest of us.

Or at least that was what the Court concluded in *Buckley v. Valeo,* the decision that ruled unconstitutional any limit on the amount of money a federal candidate could spend on his campaign, whether the money is his own or donated to him, on the ground that a limit would abridge the candidate's right to free speech.

In 1974, Congress passed a set of amendments to the Federal Election Campaign Act that placed the spending limits on federal candidates. No sooner was it passed, though, than an unlikely assortment of politicians and civil libertarians, including New York Republican Senator James Buckley, presidential candidate Eugene McCarthy, and the New York Civil Liberties Union filed suit against the new law saying it restricted their political speech because, they claimed, "virtually all meaningful political communications in the modern setting involve the expenditure of money."

A U.S. Court of Appeals upheld the law, arguing that the country had a responsibility to limit the political power of the wealthy relative to the rest of the population. "It would be strange indeed," Judge J. Skelly Wright wrote, "if . . . the wealthy few could claim a constitutional guarantee to a stronger political voice than the unwealthy many because they are able to give and spend more money, and because the amount they give and spend cannot be limited."

But the Brethren didn't find it strange at all. The Court ruled that limiting a candidate's spending "reduces the quantity of expression by restricting the number of issues discussed, the depth of their exploration, and the size of the audience reached." In short, money is equivalent to speech, and is therefore inviolable.

But if money is speech, then limits on political contributions should also be unconstitutional. Even bribery must be allowed. "I should be able to give money in exchange for a vote on a particular bill," says American University law professor Jamin Raskin. "I'm only speaking. And if someone else can offer more money, he's just speaking more eloquently."

The undemocratic effect of the Court's ruling has never been more apparent than it is today. Unchecked, any candidate can dig deep into his own pocket or what he can raise from PACs to appear as a latter-day Demosthenes. Huffington, the California multimillionaire who spent $5.4 million of his own fortune to win a seat in the House of Representatives in 1992, is expected to shell out a record $25 million challenging Senator Dianne Feinstein this year. That dwarfs the previous record of $17.7 million held by Jesse Helms, who needed every penny to ward off challenger Harvey Gantt in 1990.

Helms and Huffington wouldn't be so extravagant if they didn't think it would do some good, and they're right. Candidates who outspend their opponents almost always win their elections. According to the Center for Responsive Politics, candidates in 1992 who outspent their opponents won more than 85 percent of the time. It's no wonder that campaign spending is snowballing. As one candidate spends more, his or her opponent is in turn forced to cozy up to PACs and wealthy political patrons. The price of participating in the political process climbs ever higher. Campaign spending for 1992 jumped 52 percent from two years earlier and with Ollie North and Huffington leading the way, 1994 is shaping up to be much the same. The deafening sound you hear is not the free exchange of political ideas, but the trampling of the democratic process. Oink.

MASSIAH v. U.S., 1964

Herald "High" Price Fahringer likes this decision a lot.

"A man has been indicted, and the government takes a confederate and induces him to go to this man and take [self-incriminating] statements. That, in its nature, is very shocking," he says.

It's no wonder he feels the way he does. Fahringer is a mob lawyer, and one of the best. He has probably handled more appeals on behalf of mobsters than any other lawyer in New York City, if not the entire country. *Massiah v. U.S.* has helped him do his job on a number of occasions.

In 1958, Winston Massiah, along with several codefendants, was arrested, read his rights, arraigned and indicted on charges related to the smuggling of three-and-half pounds of cocaine into the United States. Massiah pleaded not guilty to the charges and was freed on bail.

Shortly afterwards, Massiah was discussing the case in the car of one of his codefendants, Jesse Colson. During the conversation, Massiah made several statements indicating that he was in fact guilty. Massiah did not know, however, that Colson was cooperating with the prosecutors and had his car bugged. A federal agent sitting in a car about a block away was listening to the entire conversation.

Massiah was convicted, but his lawyers appealed on the ground that the bug represented a violation of the defendant's right to counsel, only to have the initial conviction affirmed by an appellate court. They found a more receptive welcome from the Supreme Court.

In a six-to-three decision written by Justice Potter Stewart, the Court held that federal agents violated Massiah's Fifth Amendment right not to incriminate himself, and his Sixth Amendment right to counsel.

Sound crazy? It was, but consider the context. At the time *Massiah* was being considered, the Warren Court was still riding the crest of the two most important right-to-counsel decisions of the century, *Spano v. N.Y.* in 1958, and *Gideon v. Wainwright* in 1962. In Spano, the Court reversed a murder conviction that was based on a confession obtained after eight hours of intense police interrogation. Gideon, immortalized by Anthony Lewis' book *Gideon's Trumpet,* involved a crook who had broken into a pool hall. The judge in the case denied Clarence Gideon's requests for an attorney, forcing the nearly illiterate man to defend himself. Gideon was subsequently convicted, but had it overturned after he appealed to the Court in a hand-written note describing his situation.

The two precedents are used as the foundation of Stewart's decision in *Massiah,* but you'd be hard-pressed to find similarities between the cases. First of all, Massiah was never denied counsel. He had his own attorney, and the meetings between the two were not obstructed or spied upon by federal agents in any way. At the time of the "interrogation" (as Stewart put it) Massiah had every opportunity to have his attorney with him; he simply chose not to.

The claims that Massiah should be protected under the Fifth Amendment are equally absurd. The Fifth Amendment states that a person cannot be compelled to make self-incriminating statements. But there was no threat of violence when Massiah made his statements; he made them because they were true. And the federal agents didn't compel Massiah to make them. They just made sure they were there when he did.

Massiah represents yet another obstacle to the police's efforts to convict criminals. Only one-third of reported violent crimes end with the perpetrator convicted. The rights of the accused are in place to protect the defendant from being railroaded by overzealous or outright corrupt police and prosecutors. The Warren Court, however, used these rights to handcuff police and prosecutors to the point where a criminal can reasonably expect never to see the inside of a prison cell.

D*E*SHANEY *v*. WINNEBAGO COUNTY, 1989

When the Wisconsin social worker assigned to the case of Joshua DeShaney heard he was in a life-threatening coma, she said, "I just knew the phone would ring some day and Joshua would be dead."

It's not surprising she had this premonition. Anybody who knew about Joshua's father's repeated and vicious beatings of the four-year-old could have come to the same conclusion. What is surprising is that during the two years when the caseworker had solid evidence of child abuse, she did nothing to stop it.

In January 1992, Randy DeShaney's second ex-wife (Joshua's stepmother), reported to the police that her ex-husband beat the boy regularly. The report was referred to the Wisconsin Department of Social Services, which handles all accusations of child abuse. In an interview with a social worker, Mr. DeShaney denied abusing his son, and no action was taken. One year later, Joshua was again admitted to a hospital with suspicious bruises and abrasions. This time, the hospital delayed giving Joshua back into the custody of his father and convened a panel of social workers, a pediatrician, a psychologist, a police officer, and the Winnebago County lawyer to consider the immediate danger to Joshua. Despite the unexplained injuries and DeShaney's ex-wife's charge, they decided that there was not enough evidence to take Joshua away from his father and returned the boy to his custody.

A month later, Joshua was again admitted to a hospital. No legal action was taken, but the caseworker began to make regular calls on the DeShaney household, noting on several occasions bruises, abrasions, and injuries that would indicate child abuse. That November, Joshua was again admitted to a hospital, again inspected by the caseworker, and again returned to his father's custody. Five months later, the caseworker received the call she had been expecting all along. Only Joshua was not dead, just comatose. The damage to his brain was so severe that he is expected to spend the rest of his life in a home for the severely mentally retarded.

Joshua's mother took the case to court on behalf of her son, claiming that the Wisconsin DSS was responsible for damages. She lost the case in a U.S. District Court, appealed to a Court of Appeals, and lost again. She finally appealed to the Supreme Court, where she lost one last time. Wrote Chief Justice Rehnquist: "[N]othing in the language of the Due Process Clause itself requires the State to protect the life, liberty, and property of its citizens against invasion by private actors."

But the state, through the DSS social worker, did indeed have a responsibility to remove Joshua from his father's custody. Wisconsin prescribes clear duties for the DSS. All reports of possible child abuse are supposed to be directed to the DSS caseworker. Even when Randy DeShaney's second wife reported to the police that her husband was abusing Joshua, the police, rather than arresting Randy, called the DSS. In cases of child abuse, then, the DSS assumes the role held by a police department, and therefore has the same responsibilities to protect those under its jurisdiction as the police.

As Justice Brennan's dissent, joined by Marshall and Blackmun, points out, "when a State has— 'by word and by deed' . . . —announced an intention to protect a certain class of citizens and has before it facts that would trigger protection under the applicable state law, the Constitution imposes upon the State an affirmative duty of protection"—a duty the DSS did not fulfill.

Rehnquist's decision has built a nearly insurmountable barrier to suing government officials on the ground of negligence. According to the logic in his decision, police officers are not required to stop crimes in progress, nor are firemen responsible to put out fires. Most potential negligence suits against government officials aren't even filed because DeShaney makes the government virtually unaccountable for their mistakes. Justice Blackmun, in a separate dissent, exclaimed "Poor Joshua!" He very well could have included the rest of us as well.

ELROD v. BURNS, 1976, AND BRANTI v. FINKEL, 1980

DeShaney made it nearly impossible to sue government workers when they make mistakes. Protecting them even further, Elrod and Branti make it nearly impossible to fire them as well. Together, Elrod and Branti strike at the heart of an essential element in American democracy—political patronage.

The facts of the cases are simple. In the first, Richard Elrod, a Democrat, replaced Joseph Woods, a Republican, as sheriff of Cook County, Illinois. As had been done for decades, the new sheriff fired his predecessor's political appointees and replaced them with his own. In Branti there was a similar scenario: The Rockland County (New York) public defender, Peter Branti, a Democrat, refused to reappoint assistant public defenders Aaron Finkel and Alan Tabakman, who were appointed by Branti's Republican predecessor. In each case, the Republican political appointees filed suit, claiming that firing them solely on the grounds of their political party affiliation violated their First Amendment rights.

In Elrod, the Court ruled that "nonpolicy-making, nonconfidential" employees cannot be fired for their party affiliation. In Branti, the Court went even further, ruling that even policy makers could be exempt from political firings if the official trying to remove them could not prove that party loyalty was required by the duties of the positions.

The immediate effect of the Court's decisions was to cement the positions of the outgoing Republican administration's political hirings. The petitioners in each case owed their jobs to the same system they attacked as unconstitutional. And given the difficulty in firing government employees, the justices—patronage hires themselves—basically gave these political appointees life terms. In other words, the Court was giving the patronage employees the same deal it has itself: get a job through politics then have it forever insulated from a turn of the political wheel. Who can blame them for trying to share the wealth? But there's a reason the framers of the Constitution gave the High Court lifetime tenure while leaving patronage in place. It's because a limited patronage system is necessary to the two-party political system. Its importance was perhaps never better stated than by Tammany Hall's George Washington Plunkitt:

> First, this great and glorious country was built up by political parties; second, parties can't hold together if their workers don't get offices when they win; third, if the parties go to pieces, the government they built up must go to pieces, too; fourth then there'll be hell to pay.

Patronage actually increases democracy in a given political system by allowing elected officials a freer hand in choosing their staff. Every newly elected official has an idea of what government should look like and how it should work. How is that official to realize his vision if he is saddled with people hired by an administration that held a distinctly different view of government? Without the ability to hire people who share his beliefs, an elected official's efforts to streamline, or, in the current nomenclature, reinvent government, have no chance of succeeding.

The Court seems to think that it's easy for an official to shape his or her own team. In truth, bad civil servants are harder to get rid of than termites, and far more destructive. An employee can only be fired if the supervisor can prove incompetence or insubordination before a hearing board. This is no small feat; a dismissal hearing has the potential to take on the dimensions of a full civil suit. Both sides have lawyers present their case in a process that can take months to complete. Faced with the prospects of these dismissal hearings, administrators often decide firing an employee simply isn't worth the effort. Consequently, bad workers remain in their jobs and the government's performance suffers. The patronage system offers elected officials the chance to fully implement their plans for government with subordinates who have the same political goals.

When most people think of patronage hirings they envision a mayor giving a secretarial job to his mistress, despite the fact that she can't type. But there's no reason that the same skill standards that are in place in the civil service can't apply to patronage hirings as well. Agreement on politics can come in addition to, not instead of, professional skill.

To be sure, a government of unregulated patronage hirings isn't much good either. It would never get anything done if every position was newly filled every four years. By the time an administration had things up and running, they would already be on their way out. Some apolitical civil servants are vital to efficient government for the sake of continuity, just as a competence-respecting patronage system is vital for an official's ability to implement his own policy. A balance between the two must be maintained.

Why could the Court only see the evils of patronage, and not its benefits? The best answer to date comes from Mickey Kaus, who noted in a 1980 *Monthly* article on Branti that Supreme Court justices tend to be what Oliver Wendell Holmes called Jobbists. Jobbists believe that a person can check his beliefs at the door of his office, and pick them up again on his way home. Lawyers are the ultimate Jobbists, because their fundamental duty is to protect the interests of their client, no matter what. Even if a defense attorney knows his client is guilty, he still has a responsibility to defend him as best he can. Enforcing that view, the Court has staunchly upheld the Hatch Act, which prohibits political activity on the part of government workers. One's political beliefs, according to the Court's formula, are reduced to the importance of, say, one's taste in literature—personally significant, but professionally irrelevant.

This leaves a bureaucracy full of workers with no other incentive than personal advancement. The notion that these people will work with as much determination as someone who feels a sense of commitment to a greater purpose is wrong. If an individual's political beliefs have no place in government, then where do they have a place?

In his dissent to Elrod, Powell acknowledged the theoretical attractiveness of banning political patronage, yet cautioned his colleagues against taking theory where it clearly does not belong. "[W]e deal here with a highly practical and rather fundamental element of our political system, not the theoretical abstractions of a political science seminar."

It is a warning that in one way or another applies to all the cases mentioned here. The current members of the Supreme Court would do well to remember it.

CRITICAL THINKING QUESTIONS

1. Summarize these five cases and explain whether or not you disagree with the author.
2. Are there any cases that you have learned about that you think should be added to this list? Explain your reasoning.

14

Domestic and Economic Policy

Social Security and Its Discontents

John Attarian

The federal Old-Age, Survivors and Disability Insurance (OASDI) program, or Social Security, is projected to founder under the burden of supporting the huge baby-boom generation's retirement. Yet despite two decades of warnings about this, nothing is being done. The saying that Social Security is the third rail of politics—touch it and you die—holds true. Realistic observers warn that action will be more difficult the longer it is deferred, but fear of the political cost imposes paralysis.

The coming threefold crisis is familiar. Because the 1945–1965 baby boom was followed by much lower fertility, when the boomers retire, the OASDI's beneficiary population will grow much faster than its taxpayer population.

Social Security's actuaries project the number of workers supporting each beneficiary to decline from 3.4 today to 2.1 in 2030. Thus, tax rates mandated under current law cannot suffice to pay current-law benefits.

Social Security's actuaries assess its long-term outlook by calculating its long-term actuarial balance—the difference between Social Security's projected stream of expenditures over the next seventy-five years and its projected stream of income plus the trust fund's initial assets. Actuarial balance is

World and I, Jan 2003, v18, i1, p251.

© 2003 News World Communications, Inc.

expressed as a percentage of "taxable payroll" (taxable labor income). The 2002 Annual Report of Social Security's board of trustees projects an actuarial deficit for 2002 to 2076 of -1.87 percent of taxable payroll.

In 2017, the actuaries project, the OASDI's costs will begin exceeding revenues. Social Security will then start liquidating its trust fund of Treasury debt, accumulated from revenue surpluses. Trust fund exhaustion is projected for 2041, after which revenues will suffice to pay 73 percent of program costs.

Beyond Social Security's demise, two other aspects of the crisis are even more important. One is unaffordability. Redeeming Social Security's trust fund will impose colossal costs. The fund's assets are projected to peak at roughly $7.2 trillion in 2026, then decline to zero by 2041. That is, the Treasury would have to raise roughly $7.2 trillion through taxes or, more likely, borrowing, over and above Social Security's own heavy taxes, in just fifteen years. This necessarily means huge budget deficits, which will starve the economy of credit and inflict economic stagnation.

The other is political trauma. Obviously, letting Social Security collapse will be politically perilous, but the options facing our politicians are also unpleasant. The massive Social Security tax increases of 1977 and '83 embittered taxpayers, and an attempt to save the OASDI through draconian tax increases will surely trigger political upheaval. Meanwhile, beneficiaries see benefits as an inviolable earned right, and many depend on Social Security.

Their reaction to deep benefit cuts is equally predictable. Tax increases, benefit cuts, or their combination, then, are politically dangerous. Knowing this, politicians procrastinate.

Social Security's expansion to almost universal coverage—with almost all elderly Americans getting benefits and almost all working Americans paying taxes and eventually collecting benefits—has created a very dangerous political situation. Virtually everyone now has a serious stake in Social Security. Never before has almost all of our population been compellingly involved in a single government program that will likely experience grave financial difficulty or even insolvency in the next few decades. Social Security, in short, has vast potential for pitting not only generation against generation but the entire population against the government, thus creating an unprecedented political crisis.

A deep root of our predicament is the misleading manner in which Social Security has been depicted to the public by its administrators and sympathizers. This misrepresentation has generated what I call a false consciousness, that is, an understanding significantly at variance with reality but which is taken as true and governs conduct. Specifically, Social Security has been portrayed as insurance under which taxpayers pay insurance premiums or contributions to buy old age benefits, with their contributions being held in a trust fund that will pay guaranteed benefits as a matter of earned right, as America keeps its compact (or contract) between the generations.

The entire previous sentence is demonstrably, documentably false. Yet the false consciousness it summarizes decisively shaped policymaking for Social Security and still does.

THE MAKING OF A FALSE
CONSCIOUSNESS

Social Security's image has differed radically from its realities ever since the Social Security bill was introduced in January 1935. Secretary of Labor Frances Perkins and other witnesses for the Roosevelt administration told the House Ways and Means Committee that the program would pay contractual annuities as a contractual right, adding that "by contributing, the individual worker established an earned contractual right to his annuity through his own thrift." Yet the bill contained no contract language.

The Social Security Act levied payroll taxes on the first $3,000 of annual wage income in various occupations, matched by taxes on employers. Taxes would begin in January 1937 and benefits in 1942. Each fiscal year Congress would appropriate funds to an Old-Age Reserve Account at the Treasury to pay benefits for retirees aged 65 and over. Unspent funds would be invested in Treasury debt held by the account. Beneficiaries had to be retired; employment in occupations covered by the act meant loss of benefits. A worker who reached 65 without qualifying for monthly benefits would get a lump-sum benefit. If he died before reaching 65, or after starting to receive monthly benefits, his estate would get a lump sum. In all cases, benefits would at least equal a worker's tax payments; that is, there was a money-back guarantee. Again, the act contained no contract or insurance language. However, its Section 1104 reads: "The right to alter, amend, or repeal any provision of this Act is hereby reserved to the Congress." This is nothing nefarious; Congress routinely reserves the right to modify legislation to meet changing circumstances. But it has enormous implications for the popular image of Social Security.

To complaints that the payroll tax hit lowest incomes hardest, President Franklin Roosevelt replied that "those taxes were never a problem of economics. They were politics all the way through. We put those payroll contributions there so as to give the contributors a legal, moral, and political right to collect their pensions and their unemployment benefits.

With those taxes in there, no damn politician can ever scrap my Social Security program."[1]

Roosevelt's words reveal the payroll tax as a main source of the false consciousness and thus of Social Security's crisis. The payroll tax was not about financing a program but about creating a sense of entitlement to benefits as an earned right, by giving it an apparent basis in reality.

Moreover, it gave each generation of taxpayers a stake in Social Security's survival, so as to recover their money. Upon becoming elderly, each generation would see to it that the next generation paid its taxes to finance their benefits. As Roosevelt foresaw, the payroll tax made Social Security untouchable. He did not foresee that it helped trap Social Security by making benefit cuts unthinkable, forcing Congress to meet financial crises with tax increases and then, after these proved unpopular, sheer evasion.

After Congress passed Social Security, Secretary Perkins and Social Security Board chairman Arthur Altmeyer promoted the new program in the media, telling the public that benefits would be "earned annuities to which the recipients are entitled as a matter of right" and that benefits "under the Federal old-age insurance system will be paid as a matter of right to qualified individuals who have been paying their contributions . . . just as they would receive benefits from a private insurance company to which they had paid premiums."[2]

In 1937, the *Helvering v. Davis* case challenged Social Security's constitutionality. In its arguments, the government asserted that Social Security's benefits were "gratuities (not based on contract, but based on a Congressional direction expressly subject to amendment or repeal)," that its taxes were "true taxes, their purpose being simply to raise revenue," and that the act "does not constitute a plan for compulsory insurance within the accepted meaning of the term 'insurance'." All this obviously contradicts the version presented to the public.

After *Helvering v. Davis* upheld Social Security, its marketing as insurance resumed. The program's mass-consumption literature was rewritten, with "Federal Old-Age Benefits," for instance, becoming "Federal Old-Age Insurance." The media uncritically echoed this description, further disposing Americans to see Social Security as insurance. In 1939, for example, *Time* magazine described Social Security as "the biggest, most comprehensive, most expensive mass insurance policy ever written."

In response to pressure to liberalize it, Social Security was amended in 1939 to add benefits for survivors (widows and orphans) of deceased wage earners, begin benefit payment in 1940 rather than 1942, and increase benefits. To contain costs, the lump-sum death benefit was reduced and the money-back guarantee was removed. This revealed the "earned right" as malleable—something never disclosed to the public by Social Security's publications.

The amendments powerfully reinforced the insurance image by labeling Social Security "Old-Age and Survivors Insurance" and its taxes "insurance contributions." They created a new myth, too. The Old-Age Reserve Account had prompted bitter controversy. Critics, such as 1936 Republican presidential candidate Alfred "Alf" Landon, charged that the surplus held as Treasury debt in the reserve account was bogus. The government was just spending Social Security taxes on general expenses and issuing itself an IOU; people would have to be taxed again to pay the benefits. Some even accused the government of embezzling the money. The amendments redesignated the reserve account the "Old-Age and Survivors Insurance Trust Fund." Altmeyer testified before the Senate Finance Committee that this was done "to allay the unwarranted fears of some people who thought Uncle Sam was embezzling the money." The trust fund, then, was simply a Treasury account labeled as a trust fund— a public relations move meant, like the payroll tax, to shape belief.

With Social Security's label as insurance now written into law, a massive marketing campaign ensued. Numerous government pamphlets described Social Security as an insurance plan, and the payroll tax as "a sort of premium on what might be called an insurance policy." Tax money, the public was told, went into the "'Federal Old-Age and Survivors Insurance Trust Fund.' Old-age insurance benefits will be paid out of this fund." Moreover, "because the worker has helped to pay for his benefits, they come to him and his family as a matter of right." Again, the press concurred, referring to policyholders and writing of the amended act: "In effect, it writes insurance policies guaranteeing to pay monthly benefits, [which were] available as a matter of right." Taxes were labeled premiums, and so on.

THE FALSENESS OF THE FALSE
CONSCIOUSNESS

Yet the analogy to insurance was dubious. In 1953 a House Ways and Means subcommittee, headed by Congressman Carl T. Curtis (R-Nebraska), held hearings investigating Social Security. Under intense questioning from Curtis, Altmeyer made several damaging revelations. There was no insurance contract, benefit rights were malleable, and the Social Security Administration had never deemed it necessary to tell the public that Congress reserved the right to modify the Social Security Act.

Insurance scholars, meanwhile, divided over whether Social Security was insurance. Insurance copes with risk (uncertainty regarding a loss) by combining risk pooling and risk transfer. Risk pooling involves a large number of persons, each facing an uncertain, large loss, sharing the loss by each paying a certain, small charge (premium) to create a fund for compensating those members who do suffer the loss insured against. Risk transfer shifts the cost to the insurer, who invests the premiums to generate income to meet contractual obligations; if the insurer miscalculates probabilities of the risk eventuating, it risks financial loss, perhaps even bankruptcy. Social Security, its partisans argued, is "social insurance," an attempt to protect vulnerable persons from risks through government. Since social insurance spreads risk over large numbers of persons through taxes and has the same purpose as private insurance—"mutual protection against widespread risks"—it has the fundamental characteristics of insurance. Therefore, they concluded, Social Security is insurance. Critics responded that unlike private insurance, social insurance is compulsory and lacks both contracts and advance funding to meet its obligations.

The truth is, Social Security is not and has never been insurance. It lacks the defining characteristics of insurance: risk pooling and risk transfer. Benefit levels are determined by politics and ideology—for example, President Lyndon Johnson's desire to be generous to the elderly in 1967, and the election-year competition between President Richard Nixon and congressional Democrats in 1972 to increase benefits—and then taxes are raised to cover projected costs. This has nothing to do with risk; so calling such politically driven taxation risk pooling is untenable. As for risk transfer, Social Security assumes no risk whatsoever. Should it be unable to pay benefits, it will simply borrow, or Congress will raise taxes. The risk is transferred not to Social Security but to the taxpayers. The conclusion is inescapable: Social Security is income redistribution, not insurance.

The Supreme Court's decision in *Flemming v. Nestor* (1960) dramatically revealed the falseness of the false consciousness. The 1954 Social Security amendments authorized benefit termination for persons deported for subversive activity. In 1956 Ephram Nestor, deported for being a communist in the 1930s, lost his benefits. He sued, citing repeated statements by President Dwight Eisenhower and other politicians that Social Security benefits are an "earned right" and a "statutory right." That is, Nestor was demanding that Social Security live up to its advertising.

The U.S. District Court for the District of Columbia upheld Nestor. Appealing to the Supreme Court, the Justice Department, in a brief filed on behalf of Health, Education and Welfare Secretary Arthur Flemming—meaning, of course, on behalf of the Social Security Administration—demolished the image of Social Security confected for public consumption: "The OASI [Old-Age and Survivors Insurance] program is in no sense a federally-administered 'insurance program' under which each worker pays premiums over the years and acquires at retirement an indefeasible right to receive for life a fixed monthly benefit, irrespective of the conditions which Congress has chosen to impose from time to time." The Social Security tax is "not comparable to a premium under a policy of insurance promising the payment of an annuity."

Terms such as insurance, property, and vested rights "can be applied only at the risk of a serious distortion of language." This being so, the view "that such benefits are 'fully accrued property rights' is wholly erroneous." Clearly, one's right to benefits is statutory, conditional, and malleable. This was not what the public had been reading in the Social Security booklets and the press for a quarter century.

The Supreme Court decided against Nestor. In the Court's opinion, Justice John Harlan declared that the "noncontractual interest" of a Social Security taxpayer "cannot be soundly analogized to that of the holder of an annuity, whose right to benefits is bottomed on his contractual premium payments." Because Social Security depends on necessarily inaccurate economic predictions, it has to be capable of modification. Thus, the opinion held, "To engraft upon the Social Security system a concept of 'accrued property rights' would deprive it of the flexibility and boldness in adjustment to ever-changing conditions which it demands." So much for the earned right!

Harlan was correct; Congress simply has to be free to modify Social Security if circumstances change. But this means that Social Security's self-promotion was inaccurate and misleading.

POLICYMAKING IN THE SHADOW
OF MYTHS

Nevertheless, the misunderstanding flowing from that self-promotion decisively shaped the actions taken when Social Security faced financial crisis in the 1970s and '80s.

An error in the formula for calculating annual cost of living adjustments (COLAs), which were introduced in 1975, resulted in double adjustment of benefits for inflation. Combined with the 1973–75 inflationary stagnation, this meant that for the first time Social Security faced financial ruin. The Carter administration proposed covering revenue shortfalls with general revenue, but this plan was rejected since its departure from payroll tax financing would dilute Social Security's "earned right" psychology.

With no choice but to raise payroll taxes, in 1977 Congress passed, and President Jimmy Carter signed, legislation correcting the COLA error and inflicting the largest tax increase in history until then. Whereas earlier legislation had set the maximum income subject to tax at $18,900 in 1979, $20,400 in 1980, and $21,900 in 1981, the 1977 amendments raised these amounts to $22,900, $25,900 and $29,700 respectively, with automatic increases after 1981. The tax rate also jumped, from 4.95 percent of taxable labor income to 5.70 percent by 1985 and 6.2 percent by 1990. Taxpayers pelted Congress with angry mail, and polls revealed dwindling confidence in Social Security.

Despite the higher taxes, by 1981 the OASDI was again in crisis. President Ronald Reagan proposed, among other things, cutting early retirement benefits from 80 percent of the basic benefit available at age 65 to 50 percent of it. Reagan's proposals ignited an explosion of rage, proving that the false consciousness had a powerful grip on the minds of politicians and the public. "Social Security represents a compact between a worker, his employer, and the Federal Government," declared Congressman Jonathan Bingham (D–New York). "The Reagan proposals, if enacted, would tear that compact asunder. Benefits are a right—an earned right." "These are contracts we have made with our people, with ourselves—a social contract," echoed Sen. Daniel Patrick Moynihan (D–New York). Advertisements in the United Auto Workers magazine *Solidarity* declared, "Social Security Is a Contract, Not a Handout!" In letters to the editor, newspaper readers wrote such things as "Social Security is an insurance program" and "the establishment of the Social Security system embodies much that can be found in contract law." As a result, Reagan suffered his first defeat in Congress.

In 1983 Congress rescued Social Security again. It accelerated the 1977 law's scheduled tax increases, introduced benefit taxation for retirees with higher incomes (which is equivalent to cutting their benefits), and gradually raised the retirement age—the age at which one can retire with full benefits—for future beneficiaries, from 65 to 66 in 2009 and 67 in 2027. Postponement of eligibility for full benefits is, of course, a benefit cut. Early retirement benefits would still be available at age 62 but would be gradually cut from 80 percent of full benefits to 70 percent. Thus, most of the cost of saving Social Security was put on younger Americans, who had their taxes raised and their future benefits cut. The latter facts necessarily reveal the earned rights to be fictive. The compact or contract is subject to unilateral breach and revision by one party, Congress, which can compel adherence to the new version by the other parties—something not true of real contracts.

Reagan's rout demonstrated the hazards of cutting Social Security benefits guarded by a powerful constituency steeped in a false consciousness. The lesson took. Although huge budget deficits plagued the 1980s and '90s, beneficiaries were spared any real sacrifices. The 1985 Gramm-Rudman-Hollings Act, which sought to eliminate deficits by 1991 by applying automatic spending cuts if its deficit targets were missed, exempted Social Security. Attempts to eliminate the 1986 Social Security COLA and delay the COLA after the 1987 stock market crash both failed. Social Security was exempted from the 1990 Budget Enforcement Act's spending limits.

When in January 1993 the Clinton administration proposed freezing Social Security COLAs, Moynihan called the plan unacceptable. "I would like to see us acknowledge that this is a contributory insurance program," said Moynihan. "These moneys are held in trust. . . . It's paid-up insurance." Reversing himself, President Bill Clinton assured leaders of the American Association for Retired Persons that he believed Social Security was a special contract with the elderly.

Meanwhile, the tax increases were generating revenue surpluses over benefit costs. These surpluses were used to buy nonmarketable Treasury debt, as the Social Security Act has always required. Having nowhere else to go, the surplus revenue, of course, helped finance general government expenses. Since Social Security is off budget, when the government runs on-budget deficits, Social Security surpluses partly offset them. This does Social Security no injury, since its Treasury debt is redeemable through future taxing or borrowing. Yet journalists, politicians, and elderly lobbies seized upon this routine, harmless, and perfectly legal accounting phenomenon to spawn a new, pernicious myth: Congress is robbing the trust fund.

Thoroughly taken in, the American public persistently sprays its newspapers with letters railing about Congress "dipping its hands into the fund" and "borrowing and stealing from this lucrative fund." This anger, naturally, flows from the belief that Social Security's trust fund is indeed a trust fund containing money held in trust and managed by trustworthy managers on the taxpayers' behalf—precisely the belief the term was intended to induce. This totally inaccurate notion commands widespread adherence. In July 1998, Carolyn Lukensmeyer, director of the Americans Discuss Social Security project, told the Senate Special Committee on Aging that 79 percent of her respondents said spending Social Security's reserves on general government operations was one reason Social Security might have trouble in the future, and 45 percent said this was the main reason.

Social Security's public-relations campaign succeeded only too well. It and the false consciousness it created are at the very heart of our predicament. Social Security is trapped between the imperatives of politics, which force policymakers to act as if Social Security's myths are true, thus locking the program into rigidity regarding current benefits; and the imperatives of economics, which require Social Security to be flexible in order to adjust to changing conditions. Put another way, a lethal contradiction lies at Social Security's core, between the need for flexibility and the need for rigidity.

The belief that current benefits are earned rights and paid-up insurance made them virtually untouchable, so the cost of adjustment got pushed into the future, onto younger generations. This is unlikely to work any longer. The young are keenly aware of their tax burden and have little faith in Social Security.

Polls repeatedly show solid majorities of respondents opposed to any painful measure to strengthen Social Security: tax increases, benefit cuts, raising the retirement age, or means testing. With Social Security trapped between resentful taxpayers and inflexible elderly, small wonder that America is seeking to escape through Social Security reform.

REFORM: CONSTRAINED BY FALSE CONSCIOUSNESS

Social Security's defenders argue that there is no crisis. Projected program bankruptcy is decades away, and, anyway, radical reform is unnecessary. Since Social Security faces a long-term actuarial deficit of about 2 percent of taxable payroll, they argue, minor tax increases and benefit cuts totaling that amount would fix things.

Not quite. As Harry Ballantyne, Social Security's former chief actuary, explained to me, eliminating the actuarial deficit does not mean that income and expenses would balance every year—only over the entire seventy-five-year period. Early in this period, Social Security will run annual surpluses. But as baby boomer retirement drives costs above income, it will still run annual deficits in the distant future. Eliminating the actuarial deficit simply means that the trust fund's initial assets, plus the surpluses, will just cover the later deficits. Covering those deficits would still require higher taxes or borrowing from the public.

If tweaking taxes and benefits won't really solve anything, what other options are there? One widely promoted idea is privatization—complete or partial conversion of the OASDI into a system of publicly or privately held individual retirement accounts. Most of these proposals call for splitting the OASDI's tax into two tiers, one paying current retirees' benefits, the other being invested in the taxpayers' individual accounts. Others would totally replace Social Security with a system of individual accounts similar to that adopted in Chile in 1981.

As Daniel Mitchell of the Heritage Foundation observes, all privatization proposals explicitly guarantee benefits for current retirees and those near retirement.[3] Under privatization, then, workers would have to fund both their own retirements and those of existing beneficiaries. Partial diversion of payroll taxes into individual accounts would leave insufficient revenue for current benefits. This shortfall would have to be covered with general revenues or borrowing from the public. This is the problem known in the Social Security literature as "transition costs." With tens of millions of Social Security beneficiaries, transition costs would necessarily run into trillions of dollars.

Financing such huge costs will be devilishly hard. Privatizers forget that our aging population will also drive up spending for Medicare and Medicaid, which provide old-age health benefits. The Congressional Budget Office projects that Social Security, Medicare, and Medicaid spending will rise to 14.7 percent of GDP by 2030, two-thirds of the increase going to Medicare and Medicaid. These huge competing claims on the budget and economy will greatly constrain our ability to finance transition costs. As for financing the transition by borrowing from overseas, with aging populations and costly entitlement states of their own, the other developed countries will probably be unable to lend us money.

Substantially reducing transition costs would ease this problem. This can be done, however, only by substantially cutting or means-testing benefits for current beneficiaries—and here the false consciousness rears its head. One reason why privatizers insist on paying current beneficiaries all their benefits, Mitchell states, is because "the government made a contract with them to provide a certain level in exchange for taxes paid, and it would be wrong to break that contract." This, of course, is an acquiescence to the false consciousness. Because privatizers are in the toils of the false consciousness, and do not seek to break its grip on the American mind, they are doomed to wrestle with transition costs that we probably cannot carry.

Another possible Social Security reform would be reducing or eliminating benefits for higher-income retirees through means testing—that is, paying benefits based on demonstrated financial need—or steeply progressive benefit taxation. This would greatly reduce Social Security's total cost and avert a ruinous burden on the budget and economy, while skirting the risks and difficulties of privatization. Should this be proposed, however, the false consciousness would draw blood: opponents would protest that benefits are an earned right, and claim that means testing is inadmissible. Geoffrey Kollmann of the Congressional Research Service ably summed up this argument:

"Opponents see means testing as a fundamental breach of Social Security principles. Benefits have always been paid regardless of a person's economic circumstances. Means testing benefits, opponents argue, would make Social Security similar to welfare. It would weaken a primary reason for the support of the program by the public—that people believe they have paid for their benefits and are not receiving a government "handout.""

"Opponents say means testing is unfair. . . . It would break an 'implied compact' because workers paid a lifetime of taxes in the expectation of promised benefits.[4]

"It is not true that benefits have always been paid regardless of a person's economic circumstances. From the very beginning, as we saw, Social Security required retirement as a condition for benefits; income from covered employment meant loss of benefits. This retirement earnings test was enormously relaxed over time, but it is a form of means testing. Also, Congress has already broken the implied compact several times. Last but not least, the benefit taxation already enacted amounts to means testing: it cuts benefits to the better-off. Means testing does not conflict with Social Security realities, but it does collide head-on with the earned right mentality that Social Security's publicity, and its payroll tax, did so much to promote. Thus does the false consciousness cramp our reform options."

A TIME FOR TRUTH

Social Security and its partisans continue to disseminate myths. The Social Security Administration's booklet *The Future of Social Security* asserts that "for the average wage earner with a family, Social Security survivors benefits are equivalent to a $354,000 life insurance policy . . . or a $233,000 disability insurance policy." In a *Boston Globe* op-ed, Boston College professor Alicia Munnell described benefits as "established rights, promised by law." A fact sheet from the AARP and Save Our Security asserts that Social Security taxpayers "are building the earned right" to benefits. "By contributing to the system we all earn the right to receive benefits," it continues. Similarly, a fifteen-question Social Security quiz posted on AARP's Web site as of 2001 declares that benefits are "an earned right" and "since we all pay into Social Security . . . we all earn the right to protection." This after *Flemming v. Nestor*!

On September 19, 2002, I received further confirmation that the false consciousness remains alive and well. An unsolicited mailing from a group called the Council for Government Reform began: "(Washington D.C.) Senior Alert: Congress CONTINUES the Raid on the Trust Fund. . . . Trust Fund STILL headed to bankruptcy." It asked me to sign a petition demanding that Congress stop borrowing from the trust fund and guarantee Social Security and Medicare benefits from cuts. "Fact is, your Social Security benefits have BEEN EARNED and PAID FOR. They ARE NOT THE SAME as other government expenses and they should never be cut! Your petition . . . reminds [Congress] you paid for your benefits with special taxes withheld from your paychecks . . ." A brief survey accompanied, asking if I agreed that "monies paid into the Social Security Trust Fund are for payment of future Social Security checks and NOT to fund current federal spending." Did I agree that Congress "should EXCLUDE Social Security from any CUTS since Social Security is earned and paid for with special payroll taxes, unlike welfare, farm subsidies, and other so-called entitlements?"

As should by now be clear, this mailing's assertions are counterfactual. Yet millions of impressionable elderly Americans receive such mailings from senior organizations, form their beliefs about Social Security accordingly, and pressure Congress to preserve benefits intact.

Social Security is headed for serious trouble, and minor adjustments won't help much. Misleading rhetoric about insurance, contract, earned right, and trust fund still shapes thinking about Social Security and helps prevent action. Popular thinking remains dominated by the false consciousness, which is spawning new myths, such as "robbing the trust fund." If we are to achieve sound Social Security reform, we must first see Social Security as it really is, with vision unclouded by rhetoric, so we can act on the basis of facts and not fictions.

John Attarian is a freelance writer who lives in Ann Arbor, Michigan and holds a Ph.D. in economics. He has contributed several book reviews and economics articles to The World & I. *This essay is adapted from his book* Social Security: False Consciousness and Crisis, *published in September 2002 by Transaction Publishers.*

NOTES

1. Arthur M. Schlesinger Jr., *The Age of Roosevelt, vol. 2, The Coming of the New Deal* (Boston: Houghton Mifflin, 1958), 308–9.

2. Frances Perkins, "Social Security: The Foundation," *New York Times Magazine*, Aug. 18, 1935, 2, 15; A.J. Altmeyer, "The New Social Security Act," *Vital Speeches of the Day*, Oct. 7, 1935, 8–9.

3. Daniel J. Mitchell, "Creating a Better Social Security System for America," *Backgrounder 1109*, Heritage Foundation, April 23, 1997, 22.

4. Geoffrey Kollmann, "Means-Testing Social Security Benefits: An Issue Summary," Congressional Research Service, Report 94—791 EPW, 2.

CRITICAL THINKING QUESTIONS

1. What is the long-term outlook for Social Security if no changes are made?

2. What are the political difficulties involved with either raising taxes or cutting benefits?

3. What does the author mean when he refers to the "false consciousness" of Social Security?

4. Why does the author think that Social Security is in trouble?

15

Foreign and Defense Policy

The Transformation
of National Security

Philip Zelikow

FIVE REDEFINITIONS

Perhaps the key question of international politics and U.S. national security policy today is whether a genuinely new era has dawned since the end of the Cold War. It has. The attacks of September 11, 2001 did not create the new era, but they were a catalytic moment in our recognition of it. Like previous shocks to the United States in June 1940, December 1941 or June 1950, this shock gave emerging trends a form, brought them into mass consciousness, and forced upon us the task of defining a comprehensive national response.

Such a definition appears in the Bush Administration's recently published *National Security Strategy of the United States.*[1] This essay draws out some of the ideas that appear to undergird the administration's emerging strategy. It focuses on five essential redefinitions of what national security means for the United States in the 21st century—but first a note about the rhetoric of empire that has come to dominate much current discussion.

The National Interest, Spring 2003, p17, (12).

© 2003 The National Affairs, Inc.

THE DISTRACTION OF EMPIRE

All national security strategies start with a mental image of the world. The image of the new era is properly that of a modern and truly pluralistic international system. In the traditional world, populations, governance, commerce, culture and habits of life evolved slowly and changed gradually. The break point between this traditional world and that of modernity arrives, at different times for different societies, when social and technological change severs the links that had defined the relationships between humanity and the physical resources of the earth; shatters the hitherto ageless ceilings on productivity enforced by the physical limits of humans, animals, wind and water; and transforms our ability to communicate across distances, communities and nations.

These transformations acquired momentum in the 18th century and spread in the 19th until, by the year 1900, the modern world extended to Europe, North America and to their limited veins of settlement and commerce stretched out over the rest of the planet. The 20th century saw the further, nearly global extension of modernity and wrenching, worldwide efforts to adjust to its impact. Indeed, such has been the shock to many societies that the last century has been dominated by great contests over how to conceive, organize and provide moral justification and political order for modern industrial nations.

Those great contests have now subsided. The world is no longer so broken and divided. The militant utopias of class, nation and race have been defeated and discredited. Modernity means that change itself becomes the constant, and the challenge of change has not disappeared. Its pressures have instead been internalized within every society trying to adapt to a quickening pace of change. In other words, today's battle lines are less international and more transnational.

In dealing with these pressures, some see the United States as a new source of world order—fearing or welcoming that prospect. This accounts in part for the current popularity of "empire" as a reigning metaphor for America's ambitions. The metaphor is seductive, yet vicious.

What is an empire? Once upon a time, "empire" was casually applied as a positive expression, as with Jefferson's "empire of liberty." In recent years "empire" has been used to describe—often with an edge—any circumstance where a powerful country exerts influence over lesser powers, whether direct or indirect, physical, cultural or commercial. This shallow equation of all sorts of economic and cultural influences with "imperialism" was first popularized about a hundred years ago by writers reacting to Britain's war against the Boers in South Africa. John Atkinson Hobson, for example, who had an immense influence on Vladimir Lenin, condemned economic imperialism as a ruling force in the world. Hobson also worked a strong element of his anti-Semitism into his theories, seeing a cabal of Jewish bankers and merchants lurking behind Britain's excesses.

The same distasteful mixture of bad thinking was prominent after World War I. Many writers in Europe, especially in the defeated nations, decried the new "Anglo-Saxon empire" that they accused Britain and America—and the

Jews, of course—of having created.[2] The same fetid intellectual waters seep from this old gutter into much anti-American commentary today.

Sadly, even some American conservatives have joined the new anti-imperialists in seeing the United States as the metro-pole of a world empire. The appeal is understandable. After all, there is a certain gratification in imagining that one is the successor to emperors and proconsuls of past ages, a certain pleasure in opening such a dusty, venerable chest of ideas about how to sort out the affairs of faraway peoples.

But these imperial metaphors, of whatever provenance, do not enrich our understanding; they impoverish it. They use a metaphor of how to rule others when the problem is how to persuade and lead them. Real imperial power is sovereign power. Sovereigns rule, and a ruler is not just the most powerful among diverse interest groups. Sovereignty means a direct monopoly control over the organization and use of armed might. It means direct control over the administration of justice and the definition thereof. It means control over what is bought and sold, the terms of trade and the permission to trade, to the limit of the ruler's desires and capacities.

In the modern, pluralistic world of the 21st century, the United States does not have anything like such direct authority over other countries, nor does it seek it. Even its informal influence in the political economy of neighboring Mexico, for instance, is far more modest than, say, the influence the British could exert over Argentina a hundred years ago.

The purveyors of imperial metaphors suffer from a lack of imagination, and more, from a lack of appreciation for the new conditions under which we now live. It is easier in many respects to communicate images in a cybernetic world, so that a very powerful United States does exert a range of influences that is quite striking. But this does not negate the proliferating pluralism of global society nor does it suggest a will to imperial power in Washington. The proliferation of loose empire metaphors thus distorts into banal nonsense the only precise meaning of the term imperialism that we have.

The United States is central in world politics today, not omnipotent. Nor is the U.S. Federal government organized in such a fashion that would allow it to wield durable imperial power around the world—it has trouble enough fashioning coherent policies within the fifty United States. Rather than exhibiting a confident will to power, we instinctively tend, as David Brooks has put it, to "enter every conflict with the might of a muscleman and the mentality of a wimp." We must speak of American power and of responsible ways to wield it; let us stop talking of American empire, for there is and there will be no such thing.

FIVE REDEFINITIONS

The United States does have unique responsibilities as the greatest power in this pluralistic world, however. Those responsibilities have moved the Bush Administration to rethink the meaning of America's national security and it is a process of thinking that transcends yesterday's partisan differences. Both conservative and liberal orthodoxies are being challenged. To attain lasting influence, these new ideas must pass into the vocabulary and assumptions of many in both parties—just as happened with strategies of "containment" in the late 1940s and early 1950s—even as political conflict continues around the edges of this new vision.

- This vision is redefining the geography of national security.
- It is redefining the nexus between principles and power.
- It is redefining the structure of international security.
- It is redefining multilateralism.
- And it is redefining national security threats in the dimension of time.

THE NEW GEOGRAPHY
OF NATIONAL SECURITY

In the past, the geography of national security was defined by foreign frontiers. Dangerous enemies had to possess mass and scale as they first accumulated armies, navies or air forces and then deployed them. Today the frontiers of national security can be everywhere. The point is so obvious in the case of mass-casualty terrorism that it needs no elaboration.

Less obvious is the way the Bush Administration, following on but surpassing the Clinton Administration, has consistently identified poverty, pandemic disease, biological and genetic dangers, and environmental degradation as significant national security threats. All of these dangers have a transnational character, their social origins resting within the turmoil of modern and modernizing societies. In other words, national security threats in the new era are defined more by the fault-lines within societies than by the territorial borders between them. The decisive clashes in this phase of history are not therefore between civilizations but inside them.

The implications of this redefinition touch every major institution of national security in the U.S. government. We are witness to the largest Executive Branch transformation in half a century with the new Department of Homeland Security, the largest reorganization of the FBI in a generation, significant overhauling of the U.S. intelligence community, the creation of an entirely new unified command and other dramatic restructuring in the Department of Defense. Fundamental relationships between Federal, state, regional and local agencies—and the private sector—must change, and are changing, as well. These transformations are just getting under way, but they are already breaking down the core paradigm of the American national security system created in the 1940s and 1950s.

The geographical redefinition of national security profoundly affects the entire U.S. foreign policy agenda. Whether dealing with terrorism or public health, the division of security policy into domestic and foreign compartments is breaking down. U.S. foreign and security policies must delve into societies, into problems from law enforcement to medical care, in novel ways— challenging international institutions and the principles that define them to adapt. More fundamentally, if the United States is to develop national security policies that are aimed at the fault-lines within societies, those policies must transcend physical and material dimensions. They must include positions about fundamental principles.

THE NEW CENTRALITY OF MORAL PRINCIPLES

During and after World War II a conventional image of American interests developed that posed a dichotomy between realism and idealism. Practically every thinker on foreign policy alive today has grown up under the influence of this dichotomy. Realism was usually identified as a cold-eyed focus on calculations of power. Idealism embraced a pre-eminent concern for human rights, global poverty or other facets of human welfare. These two images became a convenient shorthand for labeling political factions or individual leaders. But those stereotypes, overly simple to begin with, no longer even remotely suit our times. They do not capture the nature of the controversies within the present administration, nor do they comprehend the new fusion of power and principle that is now guiding U.S. policy.

The administration's concept of a "balance of power that favors freedom"— to note the marquee concept of the National Security Strategy—applies calculations of power to the worldwide capacity to support beneficial principles affecting both relations among states and conditions within them. The administration thus emphasizes both power and a readiness to distinguish good from bad, right from wrong. The administration takes to heart the observation of John Courtney Murray that policy is the meeting-place of the world of power and the world of morality, in which there takes place the concrete reconciliation of the duty of success that rests upon the statesman, and the duty of justice that rests upon the civilized nation that he serves.[3]

The administration drives power and principle together around a remarkably straightforward statement of the "nonnegotiable demands of human dignity." Seven of these demands, all originally appearing in the President's January 2002 State of the Union message, are listed in the strategy document: the rule of law; limits on the power of the state; respect for women; private property; free speech; equal justice; and religious tolerance. All seven focus on the relationship of individuals to the state. None deals directly with the form or processes of government to produce these relationships: There is no mention here of democracy. Far from being an assertion of American exceptionalism, therefore, or a call for others to emulate the example of our "city on a hill", both the strategy document and President Bush have stressed that these are universal principles that apply everywhere. This is not an affirmation of the Scottish Enlightenment, but of human civilization itself.

Such a stance is critical in an age that seems to contradict or qualify every universal truth, preferring instead to cultivate irony as the essential human sensibility. The Bush Administration has defined one constant as the essential complement to modernity, what the National Security Strategy calls a "single, sustainable model for national success." That model features a linked conception of respect for human dignity and regard for liberating human potential. If modernity implies constant change, then greater personal and economic freedom is the perpetual safety valve, the constant source of adaptation and thus the very source of structural resilience that enables different societies to organize themselves in different successful forms. Influenced by his experiences in the Balkan crises, Tony Blair put the matter well in his October 1, 2002 speech to the Labour Party conference in Blackpool:

> Our values aren't Western values. They're human values and anywhere, anytime people are given the chance, they embrace them. Around these values, we build our global partnership. Europe and America together. Russia treated as a friend and equal. China and India seeking not rivalry but cooperation and for all nations the basis of our partnership—not power alone but a common will based on common values, applied in an even-handed way.

The Bush Administration's similar emphasis on moral reasoning, on uncomfortable (to some) judgments about good and evil, challenges some conservatives and liberals alike. The challenge to conservatives flows from the fact that traditional conservatism is founded on a cultural pessimism, on an abiding skepticism about human improvement. But President Bush (and many of his key advisors) are cultural optimists who, in their own lifetimes, have witnessed great and positive upheaval—not least the successful end to the Cold War. Indeed, President Bush's whole education reform agenda ("Leave no child behind!") epitomizes the break with traditional conservatism, and it is an attitude that carries over to world affairs. His administration's efforts on HIV/ AIDS, for example, have not bothered with the Clinton Administration's convoluted effort to justify attention to global disease in traditional national security terms. The danger is not dressed up as a threat to "stability" but is portrayed for what it really is: a moral obligation to act when tens of millions face preventable death.

The administration's rhetoric is broader still: "Including all of the world's poor in an expanding circle of development—and opportunity", the National Security Strategy states, "is a moral imperative . . . one of the top priorities of U.S. international policy." Hence the proposal for a 50 percent increase in development assistance, the largest proposed by any administration since that of John F. Kennedy. President Bush is gambling that a notoriously broken foreign aid system can be reformed to make such investments politically saleable, and perhaps thereby legitimize an even greater effort in the future.

The challenge to liberals has been more interesting, if somewhat depressing in its manifestations. The American Left in its various hues once defined itself by its fierce belief in values, a readiness to judge and to act on those judgments. It is now too often defined by dedication to a consensus that disclaims any right to make moral judgments at all—except those that condemn the U.S. government. The Left's "knowing" attitude about America's own failings has evolved into the chronic suspicion of any expression of patriotism, and into the instinctive assumption that anyone who uses words like "evil" must be some Bible-thumping rube pronouncing naive moral judgments. And to think that such a person is President of the United States!

But many liberal Democrats are now wisely pressing for a return to the ancient virtues. What, then, is the net result? One old contrarian of the Left, Christopher Hitchens wrote of it in the October 20, 2002 *Washington Post*:

> As someone who has done a good deal of marching and public speaking about Vietnam, Chile, South Africa, Palestine, and East Timor in his time (and would do it all again), I can only hint at how much I despise a Left that thinks of Osama Bin Laden as a slightly misguided and-imperialist, or a Left that can think of Milosevic and Saddam as victims. Instead of internationalism, we find among the Left now a sort of affectless, neutralist, smirking isolationism. In this moral universe, the views of the corrupt and conservative Jacques Chirac—who built Saddam Hussein a nuclear reactor, knowing what he wanted it for—carry more weight than that of persecuted Iraqi democrats.

Of course, the Bush Administration's emphasis on moral judgment is vulnerable to criticisms. One is simply aesthetic. The image of the preachy American abroad, short on talent and long on sanctimony, inspires enough resentment already, and few foreign diplomats want to encourage more such Americans to sally forth. But there are more substantive problems, too. One concerns the so-called slippery slope—and it is slippery. Yet it is hard to explain why, because one cannot right wrongs everywhere, one should not try to right them anywhere. If the United States simply deals and trades with all countries as we find them, then how, in an age when the frontiers of national security are increasingly defined by issues inside societies, can the United States take stands on the battle lines that matter most?

Then there is the problem of hypocrisy and double standards. (Saudi Arabia is of late the usual friendly villain hauled into the dock for illustration.) Here the administrations goals and rhetoric do bring with them a real burden. Whether it chooses to be reticent or outspoken, whether its reflections are offered in private or in public, any administration that stresses moral judgment is obliged to display a basic honesty about the character of other governments. And it assumes the burden of a consistent regard for the non-negotiable demands of human dignity, no matter the pull of other interests or the nation s accounts. Sometimes other strategic equities will win pride of place, and the administration should not lie to itself about the tradeoffs—either their difficulty or their durability—that will have to be made.

Confronting a messy world full of frustrating choices, President Bush might draw comfort from the remarks of another wartime president, Franklin Roosevelt:

I am everlastingly angry only at those who assert vociferously that the four freedoms and the Atlantic Charter are nonsense because they are unattainable.

If those people had lived a century and a half ago they would have sneered and said that the Declaration of Independence was utter piffle. If they had lived nearly a thousand years ago they would have laughed uproariously at the ideals of Magna Carta. And if they had lived several thousand years ago they would have derided Moses when he came from the Mountain with the Ten Commandments.

We concede that these great teachings are not perfectly lived up to today, but I would rather be a builder than a wrecker, hoping always that the structure of life is growing—not dying.[4]

THE NEW STRUCTURE OF WORLD POLITICS

Another reason for thinking hard about the centrality of moral judgment in redefining American national security is because of the way the Bush Administration, following on the work of its predecessors, is trying to integrate universal principles into great power politics. For centuries the structure of world politics has been defined by the rivalry of great powers.

It is now possible instead for the United States to form active agendas of cooperation with every major center of global power, founded on imperfect yet extraordinary degrees of agreement about underlying principles in the organization of society.

A circumstance of unprecedented great power harmony is neither an immutable fact nor a deterministic prediction. It is a contingency over which we have limited but not inconsiderable influence. Great power rivalry could return to the foreground, so present circumstances ought to be viewed as an opportunity. It is an opportunity that can be lost, however, if the Bush Administration and its successors allow serious agendas of cooperation to drift into routinized gestures and petty fractiousness. These agendas, moreover, will never be built entirely out of the bilateral relationships between the United States and other great powers. Instead, the United States must challenge its present and future partners to join in common tasks that transcend narrow concerns, offering the networks of American allies in Europe and Asia real opportunities to share the responsibilities of global leadership.[5]

In this regard, the United States and its traditional allies have already given considerable attention to Russia and China as potential great powers in transition. India, set to become not only the most populous country in the world but also its largest and most diverse democracy, deserves comparable notice. If India can balance these attributes with sustained growth and stability, the world must bring that nation, and the distinct and ancient civilization it represents, into every inner circle of global power. That would include at the least permanent representation on the United Nations Security Council and in the Group of Eight.

VARIETIES OF MULTILATERALISM

The cartoon version of America's international policy dilemma poses a choice between unilateralism versus multilateralism, the wild cowboy versus the cooperative diplomat. This depiction is false.

Everything that America does in the world is done multilaterally. That emphatically includes the policies the Bush Administration considers most important, and even those that are the most "military" in character. The global war against terrorism is being conducted through an elaborate, often hidden, network of multilateral cooperation among scores of governments. A large number of players are interacting on intelligence, law enforcement, military action, air transportation, shipping, financial controls and more. Ongoing military operations in Afghanistan involve several countries, and were multilateral even at the height of American military activity, as the United States relied heavily on relationships with Pakistan, Russia, three Central Asian governments and a variety of Afghan factions.

The caricature of the administration's unilateralism usually rests on the recitation of a by now standard list of diplomatic actions that some other governments did not like (Kyoto, the International Criminal Court and so on). Some of these disagreements were handled in a style and manner that seemed insensitive or simply maladroit. Unfortunately, too, the caricature of the administration's unilateralism is willingly fed by some U.S. officials and unofficial advisers who relish the chance to play the role of the truth teller lancing foreign obfuscations. Sometimes they overplay the part, sensing the license they get from working for a plain-spoken president.

President Bush, however, is more sensitive to foreign opinion than some who act in his name. He knows that, to much of the world, "I'm the toxic Texan, right?" He recognizes that if you want to hear resentment, just listen to the word unilateralism. I mean, that's resentment. If somebody wants to try to say something ugly about us, 'Bush is a unilateralist, America is unilateral.' You know, which I find amusing.

He finds it amusing because he meets and works with foreign dignitaries almost every day, and sees himself as a "pretty good diplomat"—though he smilingly concedes that "nobody else does." From the time Bush first started making decisions about the Iraq issue, for example, he has worked at every turn through international coalitions, noting how much he had enjoyed building one for the war in Afghanistan.[6]

Europeans, of course, rush to play the part of the cosmopolitan professional who rolls his eyes and offers wittily barbed observations about American innocents abroad. Sometimes they, too, overplay the part. But all this is a very old genre of diplomatic theater; John Adams and the Comte de Vergennes set the archetypes more than two hundred years ago. It has since been performed on many stages with a wonderful variety of scripts and sets. No doubt it will be played often in future, as well.

Beyond problems of tone and execution, the real differences in the multilateral strategies of the Bush Administration and other friendly states are not about "unilateralism" versus "multilateralism." They have to do instead with five contrasting ways of conceiving and operationalizing multilateral action.

First, the Bush Administration prefers an inductive method that draws ideas from many sources and adapts them to specific conditions. Alternative deductive strategies develop abstract principles and develop them into generic, universal solutions. For instance, the painstakingly crafted individual agreement drawn up for handling war crimes in Sierra Leone, blending local and foreign judicial traditions, is preferable to the one-size-fits-all approach taken in designing the International Criminal Court. The former is designed to solve real problems and get real results on a case-by-case basis. The latter, unfortunately, aims at more rarefied ambitions.

Second, the administration prefers international institutions that judge performance and stress accountability rather than those that maintain a detached neutrality in order to preserve a friendly consensus. Too often, for example, the institutions charged with preventing the proliferation of weapons of mass destruction seemed to choose courtesy over candor. The history of IAEA inspections in Iraq—going back to the 1970s—is exemplary.

Third, the administration prefers multilateral strategies that rely on the sovereign accountability of states instead of strategies that limit sovereignty in order to link states together in a common enterprise—but which thereby dissipate responsibility. As the European Union attempts to develop a "common foreign and security policy", it can hardly avoid a lowest common denominator approach, for example.

Fourth, the administration takes a view of international law that emphasizes democratic accountability, plainly linking the authority of international officials to constitutional sources of political authority that are essentially national in character. Other nations contemplate and encourage much broader delegation of sovereign powers, where only the initial delegation need occur through a democratic process, so that international officials can have greater freedom of action. Hence the U.S. government believes that the International Criminal Court, as a permanent yet essentially stateless entity, might grow ever more distant from the democratic sources of legitimacy that are an essential source for its claimed right to administer global justice.

Fifth, the administration prefers functional institutions that produce concrete results instead of symbolic measures that might rally more support for an ideal, but at the cost of not doing much to further its attainment.

Sometimes, as in the case of the Kyoto Accords, well-meaning but dysfunctional efforts can be worse than useless if they complicate attempts to develop a more effective and sustainable solution. We cannot afford such indulgences in a world that in some ways is more threatening today than it was during the Cold War.

REDEFINING NATIONAL SECURITY
AS A FUNCTION OF TIME

Imagine threats as having a cadence—rhythm plus speed. In the past, threats tended to emerge slowly, often visibly, as weapons were forged, armies were conscripted, units were trained and deployed, and enemy forces were massed in position to move. The greatest threats, too, came from large states that could raise and equip the mass armies of the industrial age. Precisely because of their size and elaborate structures, these large states had much to lose in a war. Doctrines of deterrence were developed to confront such states, first in the pre-nuclear and then in the nuclear age.

In today's world, threats can emerge more quickly, without having to accumulate a mass of men and metal. Nor do the greatest threats necessarily come from large states that have much to lose.[7] It is thus hard to quarrel with the essential premise of the Bush Administration's open willingness to consider pre-emption, which is that the strategic military doctrines developed for the Cold War must be adapted to the circumstances of the 21st century.

Note, too, the interaction of the new cadence of threat with the new geography of national security. The fault-lines are now inside societies, where even small political factions might have access to weapons of unprecedented destructiveness. The line between internal and international security becomes blurry in parallel with the acceleration of the cadence of threat.

The basic critique of the Bush strategy of pre-emption is that it is better to wait until threats are so acute and universally apparent that a consensus can form in favor of forceful action against them. The flaw in this argument is that there is today a kind of inverse continuum of threat and vulnerability. As a potential enemy's WMD capability becomes more threatening, it becomes less vulnerable to military disruption. Such programs are most vulnerable when they are immature, but that is when the threats they pose are so ambiguous that it is harder to rally allies to act against them. Yet at the point where such threats are so evident that coalitions readily arise, it may be too late—weapons will have already been used, programs will be difficult or impossible to destroy, or outsiders will be themselves deterred by their fear of retaliation.[8]

There is a long tradition in American history of keeping dangerous threats at bay, if necessary by pre-emptive action. Defending Andrew Jackson's pre-emptive invasion of Spanish Florida, his occupation of Pensacola and his execution of individuals inciting Seminole and Creek raids against the United States, Secretary of State John Quincy Adams informed the Spanish government that by all the laws of neutrality and of war, as well as of prudence and humanity, [Jackson] was warranted in anticipating his enemy by the amicable and, that being refused, by the forcible occupation. . . . There will need no citations from printed treatises on international law to prove the correctness of this principle. It is engraved in adamant on the common sense of mankind.

No writer upon the laws of nations ever pretended to contradict it. None, of any reputation or authority, ever omitted to assert it.[9]

More recently the United States was prepared to deal with acute dangers by taking pre-emptive or preventive military action against states with which we were technically at peace—Cuba and the Soviet Union in 1962 and North Korea in 1994—if diplomacy had failed to remove or contain specified dangers. The great debates in the Kennedy Administration were over whether or how to even give diplomacy a chance. But there is abundant evidence of President Kennedy's underlying resolve to remove the Soviet missiles from Cuba, one way or another, to prevent an even more dangerous nuclear crisis from arising the next month over Berlin. In 1993 and 1994 the Clinton Administration readied military options against North Korea with evident purpose, but President Clinton never had to make the final decision on what to do if his diplomatic gambit failed. Actually, Iraq is a less clear case of pre-emptive strategy than either of these historical examples, since the United States and the most concerned allies have been in a state of hostilities against Iraq for years.

The United States and others have long been conducting constant, if mostly low-intensity, combat operations ever since Iraq conclusively broke the terms of the 1991 military truce that suspended, but never concluded, the Gulf War.

The Bush Administration's strategy is a more explicit adaptation to the new conditions of international life. That explicitness has drawn fire from some who argue that while it might be proper to hold these views, it is not wise to call attention to them. They do not reject the administration's thinking, and can themselves list many examples of real and potential cases of pre-emption. They rather accuse the administration of tactlessness.

The new strategy is somewhat provocative, but it is deliberately so. It must be provocative if it is to foster the painful worldwide debate that must occur in order to condition the international community to think hard about these new dangers, and about how the cadence of security threats has changed. Although the debate is still raging, the older habits of thought are already changing, subtly, around the world. It remains to be seen how the argument over what is and is not tactful will ultimately be settled.

In any event, the United States has not arrogated to itself some vague right to pursue and pummel anyone it dislikes, as many critics contend. The strategy document lists five criteria that must be met for a state or an organization to cast itself outside of ordinary international protection. Condoleezza Rice observed in her Wriston lecture:

[T]his approach must be treated with great caution. The number of cases in which it might be justified will always be small. It does not give a green light—to the United States or any other nation—to act first without exhausting other means, including diplomacy. Pre-emptive action does not come at the beginning of a long chain of effort. The threat must be very grave. And the risks of waiting must far outweigh the risks of action.

Moreover, the administration's focus is not just on security threats, but also on opportunities. The terrorists have no vision of the future that can assure Muslim parents that their children will lead a better life; the United States does. There are only a few states that could start a new wave of dangerous WMD proliferation, and deflecting them now may nudge history in the right direction. Failure to do so, however, may condemn millions to needless suffering and the American people to years of living in fear.

GRAND STRATEGY AND SMALL REALITIES

The Bush Administration has helped spur worldwide debate not only about the purposes of American power, but about the objectives of the international system as a whole. The United States is not challenging the necessity of international institutions for common action, but it is pressing other nations to decide what they want, to reconsider how to get it, and to re-evaluate old habits in light of new realities. This is an uncomfortable and necessarily disruptive process, and the U.S. government is bound to add its share of distracted stumbles to its progress. But the international agenda is already changing in positive ways.

Grand strategy usually disappoints when it is carried into action. Measured against this or that phrase, this or any administration will come up short. But it is possible to offer general direction, to set different chains of action and reaction into motion. Critics of the Bush Administration's emerging ideas must either accept the new definitions of national security presented or articulate coherent alternatives, working through the implications of present—not past—realities.

There are always too many problems. But the great powers are working together more than anyone would have considered possible half a century ago. New approaches to economic and humanitarian cooperation offer great promise. The advances in human liberty and material well-being just since 1990 have been staggering enough to encourage ambitious thoughts about what might be possible. With new understandings about the real problems the United States and its friends face together, and a flexible, pragmatic approach to achieving them, the prospects have never been better for the project of building a commonwealth of freedom.

NOTES

1. This document represents a more comprehensive articulation of themes that President Bush had already begun to introduce, notably in his speeches to a joint session of Congress (September 20, 2001), on the State of the Union (January 29, 2002) and to graduating cadets at West Point

(June 1, 2002). Less well known, but displaying a related set of ideas that antedate the 9/11 attacks, were the President's remarks to the World Bank on July 17, 2001 and, subsequent to those attacks, the address to the Inter-American Development Bank on March 14, 2002 (followed eight days later by the Millennium Challenge Account initiative in Monterrey). Condoleezza Rice also added an important summary of the strategy in the Wriston Lecture she delivered in New York City on October 1, 2002.

2. See Richard Koebner and Helmut Dan Schmidt, *Imperialism: The Story and Significance of a Political Word, 1840–1960* (Cambridge: Cambridge University Press, 1964).

3. Murray, *Morality and Modern War* (New York: Council on Religion and International Affairs, 1959).

4. From an address in Ottawa delivered after the Quebec strategy conference of 1943. The language was FDR's own, added in his own hand at the end of the draft his speechwriters had prepared. Samuel I. Rosenman, *Working with Roosevelt* (London: Rupert Hart-Davis, 1952), p. 356.

5. I have elaborated. these ideas in "American Engagement in Asia", in Robert D. Blackwill & Paul Dibb, eds., *America's Asian Alliances* (Cambridge, MA: MIT Press, 2000); and "The New Concert of Europe", *Survival* (Summer 1992).

6. Quotations are drawn from Bob Woodward, *Bush At War* (New York; Simon & Schuster, 2002), pp. 44, 341–2.

7. An essential argument in Charles Krauthammer, "The Unipolar Moment Revisited", *The National Interest* (Winter 2002/03).

8. The current cases of North Korea and Iraq offer interesting illustrations. For a general consideration of preventive/pre-emptive strategies, see my essay on "Offensive Military Options", in Robert D. Blackwill & Albert Carnesale, eds., *New Nuclear Nations: Consequences for US Policy* (New York: Council on Foreign Relations, 1993).

9. Adams to Erving, November 28, 1818, in Worthington Chauncey Ford, ed., *Writings of John Quincy Adams* (New York: Macmillan, 1916), p. 483. John Lewis Gaddis called my attention to the significance of Adams' influence in the Goldman Lectures he delivered in New York City in September 2002.

Related Article: Patience, Flexibility, Intelligence

For progress there is no cure. Any attempt to find automatically safe channels for the present explosive variety of progress must lead to frustration. The only safety possible is relative, and it lies in an intelligent exercise of day-to-day judgment.

The problems created by the combination of the presently possible forms of nuclear warfare and the rather unusually unstable international situation are formidable and not to be solved easily. Those of the next decades are likely to be similarly vexing, 'only more so.' The U.S.-USSR tension is bad, but when other nations begin to make felt their full offensive potential weight, things will not become simpler.

Present awful possibilities of nuclear warfare may give way to others even more awful . . . [and] we should not deceive ourselves: once such possibilities become actual, they will be exploited. It will, therefore, be necessary to develop suitable new political forms and procedures. All experience shows that even smaller technological changes than those now in the cards profoundly transform political and social relationships. Experience also shows that these transformations are not a priori predictable and that most contemporary 'first guesses' concerning them are wrong. For all these reasons, one should take neither present difficulties nor presently proposed reforms too seriously.

The one solid fact is that the difficulties are due to an evolution that, while useful and constructive, is also dangerous. Can we produce the required adjustments with the necessary speed? The most hopeful answer is that the human species has been subjected to similar tests before and seems to have a congenital ability to come through, after varying amounts of trouble. To ask in advance for a complete recipe would be unreasonable. We can specify only the human qualities required: patience, flexibility, intelligence.

John von Neumann

"Can We Survive Technology?"
Fortune (June 1955)

Philip Zelikow is the White Burkett Miller Professor of History and Director of the Miller Center of Public Affairs at the University of Virginia. He contributed unofficially to the preparation of the National Security Strategy of the United States, but the views expressed in this article are solely his own.

CRITICAL THINKING QUESTIONS

1. Why does the author feel the United States will not create an "empire"?
2. List the five "redefinitions" and give a two- to three-sentence description of each.
3. Pick one of these "redefinitions" and either agree or disagree with it. Be sure to give supporting reasons for your opinion.

16

State and Local Government

The Dire State of the States

Amey Stone

They're mired in deficits, as are city halls—and with the federal deficit ruling out help from Washington, investors have another worry.

For a couple of weeks late last year and early in 2003, investors were able to look past all the signs of economic weakness and see a light at the end of the tunnel. Sure, consumers were flagging and corporations retrenching. But once Iraq was over with (assuming a quick and not-too-dirty fight), the theory was that federal stimulus would kick in, chief executives would dust off their capital-spending plans, and Corporate America as well as individuals would suddenly feel better about investing in the future. That was the idea, anyway.

Since then, another drag on the economy has become increasingly apparent—and passage of the Bush stimulus plan and winning a war in Iraq would do little to relieve it: the growing financial problems of state and local governments. For investors, this is yet another macroeconomic headwind to keep in mind before jumping back into the market.

After spending rainy-day funds in 2001 and 2002, and now plagued by tax receipts that continue to come in weaker than forecast, states have seen their finances deteriorate in a matter of months. In November, the two-thirds of

Business Week Online, Feb 7, 2003, pNA.

© 2003 The McGraw-Hill Companies, Inc.

states surveyed by the National Conference of State Legislatures (NCSL) projected budget shortfalls of $17.5 billion. By early February, their budget gaps had risen to $26 billion (see BW Online, 02/07/03, "State Taxes Need New Thinking"). Moody's now has a negative outlook on the credit of 17 states, which means they could be subject to downgrades in the next 12 months and face significantly higher borrowing costs.

WHAT STIMULUS? Saddled with requirements that they balance their budgets each year, states are likely to resort to raising taxes and cutting spending—both major drags on local economies. Hikes in taxes eat into discretionary spending by consumers. Cuts in spending inevitably mean layoffs. According to the NCSL, at least 24 states are considering tax-increase proposals, 12 states have cut higher education, and 9 have laid off state employees.

"By increasing taxes at the state level, everything Bush offers as fiscal stimulus is going to be more than offset," says Robert Smith, economist and president of fixed-income investment firm Smith Affiliated Capital. Many of these financial problems will inevitably get handed down to municipal governments, which will do things like hike fees and raise property taxes, also eating into consumers' discretionary income.

Even more worrisome for the long-term health of state and local economies, governments are resorting to measures like cutting education and health care, even shortening prison terms as a way to save money. That can hurt a state's long-term economic performance, says William Gale, an expert in tax and fiscal policy at the Brookings Institution. He thinks the best thing Congress could do now to stimulate the economy is provide states with additional aid. But with the federal budget deficit already soaring beyond expectations, that kind of help probably isn't politically feasible in the near term.

AGE OF ANXIETY. Policy experts as well as professional investors have long anticipated local governments' financial problems would worsen in 2003. But the magnitude of the economic impact is just becoming clear, now that governors and legislators are unveiling budget proposals and proposing painful cuts and tax increases. "We've all known it's out there, but people are just coming to grips with it," says Stephen Carpenter, who manages tax-free bond portfolios for Cleveland-based National City Investment Management.

For investors, the coming months of budget wrangling will add to the general climate of anxiety and uncertainty, says Trip Jones, a senior vice-president at investment firm Fulcrum Global Partners. For example, as a commuter into New York City, he worries that he may be subject to the huge hike in commuter taxes proposed by New York City Mayor Michael Bloomberg. "I'm saying to myself, 'How much are my state taxes going to go up? Is Bloomberg going to get me?'" says Jones. "It's that uncertainty that freezes you and creates inaction."

Beyond the macroeconomic effects, investors in tax-free bonds will feel the pinch of the ongoing squeeze on state budgets. "Obviously there's going to be more municipal debt, which means more supply on the market, which drives down prices and raises yields," says National City's Carpenter. The end result: Muni bonds on average are getting riskier.

TIME TO BUY? While some of this has already been factored into muni-bond prices, the market seems to be waiting to see how specific states deal with their own budget issues before reacting, says Eric Kelley, who manages fixed-income portfolios for UMB Trust Investments in Kansas City, Mo. "I haven't seen yields get pushed up in a meaningful way in response to this yet," he says. And so far, he doesn't expect any states to have major credit problems. Says Kelley: "What we're worried about is that a lot of this could get pressed downstream to local cities and counties."

Perversely, Smith believes municipal bonds are actually the most attractive area of the market right now, partly because inflation is so low and also because yields are high on an aftertax basis. But he suggests avoiding general-obligation bonds, which are paid out of tax receipts, and instead considering revenue issues (bonds for things like water and sewer or electric projects), since they have their own revenue streams and are safer. Either way, diversification across states and issues makes more sense than ever, says Kelley.

The broader economic drag of looming state tax hikes and budget cuts are tougher to diversify against. There may still be a light at the end of the tunnel for the economy and the stock market if conflict with Iraq can be resolved and some sort of fiscal stimulus package makes it through Congress. But the states' mounting fiscal woes are one reason that light isn't burning very bright right now.

CRITICAL THINKING QUESTIONS

1. Summarize the difficulties that states are facing with their budgets and the impact that this might have. On your own, research how the financial health of states may have changed since this article was written.

InfoMarks: Make Your Mark

What Is an InfoMark?

It's a single-click return ticket to any page, any result, any search from InfoTrac College Edition.

An InfoMark is a stable URL, linked to InfoTrac College Edition articles that you have selected. InfoMarks can be used like any other URL, but they're better because they're stable—they don't change. Using an InfoMark is like performing the search again whenever you follow the link—whether the result is a single article or a list of articles.

How Do InfoMarks Work?

If you can "copy and paste," you can use InfoMarks.

When you see the InfoMark icon on a result page, its URL can be copied and pasted into your electronic document—Web page, word processing document, or email. Once InfoMarks are incorporated into a document, the results are persistent (the URLs will not change) and are dynamic.

Even though the saved search is used at different times by different users, an InfoMark always functions like a brand new search. Each time a saved search is executed, it accesses the latest updated information. That means subsequent InfoMark searches might yield additional or more up-to-date information than the original search with less time and effort.

Capabilities

InfoMarks are the perfect technology tool for creating:

- Virtual online readers
- Current awareness topic sites—links to periodical or newspaper sources
- Online/distance learning courses
- Bibliographies, reference lists
- Electronic journals and periodical directories
- Student assignments
- Hot topics

Advantages

- Select from over 15 million articles from more than 5,000 journals and periodicals
- Update article and search lists easily
- Articles are always full-text and include bibliographic information
- All articles can be viewed online, printed, or emailed
- Saves professors and students time
- Anyone with access to InfoTrac College Edition can use it
- No other online library database offers this functionality
- FREE!

How to Use InfoMarks

There are three ways to utilize InfoMarks—in HTML documents, Word documents, and email

HTML Document

1. Open a new document in your HTML editor (Netscape Composer or FrontPage Express).
2. Open a new browser window and conduct your search in InfoTrac College Edition.
3. Highlight the URL of the results page or article that you would like to InfoMark.
4. Right click the URL and click Copy. Now, switch back to your HTML document.
5. In your document, type in text that describes the InfoMarked item.
6. Highlight the text and click on Insert, then on Link in the upper bar menu.
7. Click in the link box, then press the "Ctrl" and "V" keys simultaneously and click OK. This will paste the URL in the box.
8. Save your document.

Word Document

1. Open a new Word document.
2. Open a new browser window and conduct your search in InfoTrac College Edition.
3. Check items you want to add to your Marked List.
4. Click on Mark List on the right menu bar.
5. Highlight the URL, right click on it, and click Copy. Now, switch back to your Word document.
6. In your document, type in text that describes the InfoMarked item.

7. Highlight the text. Go to the upper bar menu and click on Insert, then on Hyperlink.
8. Click in the hyperlink box, then press the "Ctrl" and "V" keys simultaneously and click OK. This will paste the URL in the box.
9. Save your document.

Email

1. Open a new email window.
2. Open a new browser window and conduct your search in InfoTrac College Edition.
3. Highlight the URL of the results page or article that you would like to InfoMark.
4. Right click the URL and click Copy. Now, switch back to your email window.
5. In the email window, press the "Ctrl" and "V" keys simultaneously. This will paste the URL into your email.
6. Send the email to the recipient. By clicking on the URL, he or she will be able to view the InfoMark.